FROM
LEARNER
TO EARN£R

A recruitment
insider's guide for
students wanting to
achieve graduate
job success

SOPHIE MILLIKEN

RETHINK PRESS

First published in Great Britain in 2019 by Rethink Press
(www.rethinkpress.com)

Cover image © HappyAprilBoy | Shutterstock

Praise

'Sophie's wealth of experience flows from every page in this book. Too many students spend too little time focused on their career. Full of practical advice and insider tips, this book will help students at every stage of their career journey: from deciding where to start, to navigating the selection process, to making the right impression on day one. *From Learner to Earner* is as comprehensive as the title suggests.'
— **Stephen Isherwood**, Chief Executive, Institute of Student Employers

'Sophie has a wealth of knowledge about the graduate recruitment process built up over many years working with students, employers and universities. Her book will take you on a journey that starts with your first tentative questions, travels through the application and selection process, and continues all the way on to making a great impression in your first job, with plenty of hints, tips and resources to help you stay on track. If you are a student or a graduate looking to start your job search, this book should be your first step.'
— **Gary Argent**, Managing Director, Graduate Transitions Limited

'Whether you are conducting your own search for a graduate job, or helping someone else who is, *From Learner to Earner* is a must-read. Sophie's practical and sensible advice is based on her considerable experience of graduate recruitment, both as an in-house recruiter and as an award-winning recruitment business owner, and helps to demystify the whole process. Following her recommendations will help you stand out from the crowd.'

— **Kay Jones**, Assistant Director (Business Engagement, Marketing and Events) Careers Service, Newcastle University, and Chair of the Institute of Student Employers Steering Group (Scotland and the North)

'There can be few people better placed than the author to prepare students for the job market that faces them. Sophie's knowledge of the subject is superseded only by her passion and enthusiasm. *From Learner to Earner* is an excellent navigational tool and must-have companion for students as they begin in earnest to look beyond the academic years.'

— **Machar Smith**, Recruitment Manager APAC, dunnhumby

'Sophie has created a book that should be every student's bible to navigate their way through university life and ensure they focus on getting a great graduate job at the end of their studies. Sophie has managed to bring together everything you could ever need to know about the world of graduate recruitment and, if you follow her advice, you will be in a great position to leave university with the job of your dreams.'

— **Gemma Hurt**, Early Careers Leader, GE Aviation

'*From Learner to Earner* is the must-read guide for students seeking a successful career. The book is packed with useful case studies, insightful perspectives from employers and plenty of practical tips from recruitment experts. Whether students are exploring their strengths or planning how to impress in their first job, Sophie Milliken's book is an essential guide. Milliken takes us on a fascinating journey, from discovering the UK graduate recruitment market to securing a mentor in the workplace. She shares her first-hand experiences, as well as case studies from the hundreds of students she has worked with throughout her career. Clear, structured, succinct and full of insight, this is recommended reading for every student looking to start their career journey in the UK.'

— **Enri Cocchi**, Career Development Lead and Career Coach, London Business School

'Sophie's book is one I wish I could give to all of our students upon arrival. It provides expert advice written in a friendly accessible manner, covering all aspects of career planning and job search no matter what stage in the process the student is at. It's full of useful tips and handy templates to encourage action.'
— **Judith Baines**, Head of Careers and Employment Service, University of Hertfordshire

'This is the go-to guide for any student looking to be successful in finding their chosen graduate role. In an increasingly competitive graduate job market, Sophie's clearly structured, practical guidance and expert tips are highly relevant for students from all degree disciplines. *From Learner to Earner* will allow students to impress throughout the assessment process and onwards into the working environment, so that they get their career off to a winning start.'
— **Chris Barlow**, Lecturer, University of Liverpool

'As a graduate, the main challenge I have faced is presenting the best version of myself to prospective employers. By providing crucial insights from the employer perspective, Sophie has created a resource for turning that job application into a job offer. You will develop an understanding of how to negotiate each stage of the process from CV through to final interview, ensuring you put your best foot forward. For a "how to" guide on securing that dream job, you need look no further.'

— **Joshua Silver**, recent graduate

'Today's undergraduate needs a disciplined approach to securing a graduate job and *From Learner to Earner* will provide students with clear and concise guidance to help them with every step of the process. The book will also be invaluable to the increasing number of students looking to obtain a placement during their time at university. Sophie's experience and insight into the graduate recruitment process is extensive, and this book allows all students the opportunity to access this wealth of knowledge and help them be successful in their graduate job search.'

— **Gary Dewey**, Associate Professor in Accounting, Durham University Business School

'This is a must-read for any student who wants recruitment success! Sophie covers everything to help the next generation of talent be successful in their career endeavours and progression. This is a practical toolkit for any student who wants to transition from study to employment.'

    — **Tonia Galati**, Head of Employability Engagement UK, ACCA – Europe and Americas

Contents

Foreword

From a candidate wearing swimming trunks and goggles during a video interview, to an application for a job at Marks & Spencer arriving in a box with a pair of Primark shoes, in the last twelve years of being involved in graduate recruitment, I've pretty much seen it all. People have always wanted to stand out from the rest during the application and assessment journey. These days, with an average of seventy-five applications for every graduate position, you'd be forgiven for thinking that this has become more critical than ever. But here's the good news: you don't need to come up with the wildest and wackiest idea to get noticed and be successful.

With so many students focusing their efforts on obtaining their degree to realise that return on their significant investment, the prospect of navigating the jobs market and securing that first step on the career ladder can be overwhelming. First, there's the significant time investment required for the application process, often all via online tests designed to screen people out, followed by the daunting prospect of attending an assessment centre and a series of simulation exercises – it's enough to make even the most resilient of students question themselves. But there are plenty of ways to stand out and secure that role without having to dust off your diving gear.

I first met Sophie twelve years ago, when we worked in similar graduate recruitment roles for John Lewis and Marks & Spencer respectively. We worked collaboratively with other retail organisations, which were also recruiting graduates, as part of a retail sector group within the Association of Graduate Recruiters (now the Institute of Student Employers). We all shared a common goal and experienced similar challenges – so despite being competitors in the corporate arena, it was great to come together to drive initiatives and deliver events for students and careers advisors alike. These initiatives and events were designed to dispel myths – such as those who talk most at an assessment are the most successful – and to help people navigate the application and selection journey. Sophie successfully led John Lewis to be recognised as one of the best destinations in the UK for graduates, and during that time, we often collaborated and shared insights and best practices. Being a graduate recruiter can be a lonely job – we're often the only one of our kind within an organisation – so Sophie quickly established herself as one of my most trusted 'phone-a-friend' lifelines. Her experiences, knowledge and insight have proven invaluable over the years. She has supported my decisions, clarified the directions I've taken and been a great sounding board.

I continued to work with Sophie as she started her own business, Smart Resourcing Solutions. The opportunity to partner with a supplier who really understood and could navigate the graduate recruitment industry, and support me with the design and delivery of assessment solutions as we developed new programmes, was invaluable. Sophie now works across the university sector and with a wide range of employers driving employability courses and developing assessment solutions.

There are so many books out there written from the perspective of a careers advisor, but this book offers its readers unique insight and guidance from the perspective of someone who has been specifically attracting and recruiting graduates for the last fifteen years.

From Learner to Earner will guide you through each stage of the graduate job application process – from identifying what you want to do and determining what you're good at, to understanding how to convey this in the best way to prospective employers – and share hints and tips which will give you more confidence to secure the job of your dreams.

Good luck.

Helen Alkin, MCIPD, Head of Emerging Talent Strategy and Resourcing at British Airways and a board director at the Institute of Student Employers

Introduction

As a student in your final year, or a recent graduate, you don't know what you don't know in order to find and achieve your ideal job, so you need a graduate recruitment expert. A former graduate recruiter at John Lewis, I'm now managing director at a graduate recruitment and employability consultancy, and I work with a variety of employers and universities. I am that expert.

Supporting graduates in what could be the first and most important step in their career is really important to me. Seeing graduates doing meaningful work they love is hugely rewarding and also supports the work I do with employers to help them assess candidates effectively. When students understand and can showcase their strengths and values, they can then match these to a fantastic opportunity with an employer. My passion to see every student and graduate given the skills and knowledge they need to secure their dream job after university drives much of the work I do and has led me to write this book.

The challenge

Data shared by the Institute of Student Employers (ISE) showed an average of forty-one applications for every graduate job in 2018.[1] The ISE Student Development Survey 2019 also states that 'although graduates are the biggest group of employees (52%) and their numbers have increased by 9% since 2016, the trend across the last three years suggests that the number of non-graduate entrants to these firms is increasing more rapidly with apprentices increasing by 56% and school and college leavers by 20%'.[2] The cost of obtaining a degree is higher than ever. And with increased competition from other avenues, such as apprenticeship programmes, it can feel that securing a graduate job is harder than ever.

As a student, you want to get a good degree to see a return on your investment of fees. You're also likely to have a job (or two!) and might be involved in extracurricular and social activities as well. In your final

1   Hooley, T (2018) *ISE Annual Student Recruitment Survey 2018.* https://ise.org.uk/page/ISEPublications, p8.
2   Hooley, T (2019) *ISE Student Development Survey 2019.* https://ise. org.uk/page/ISEPublications, pv.

year, you may be panicking to submit a dissertation which achieves the holy grail of the 2:1 or above. All these factors often lead students to graduate without having a graduate job lined up.

Whether you're a proactive student looking to have a job offer under your belt before graduation or a recent graduate feeling as if you've missed the boat, *From Learner to Earner* will show you exactly what you need to learn and do to secure the graduate job of your dreams.

The graduate job market can seem daunting. With such scary application numbers per job and so much competition, is there any point in applying? Where do you even start? Don't be put off by the statistics. You can land a great job. And if you get organised, you can even do this before you leave university.

As a graduate recruitment expert with over fifteen years of experience, I'll cut through the theory and provide you with a clear sense of what you're good at and how to succeed during the assessment process. I'll give you the knowledge and tools you need to impress your dream employer.

From Learner to Earner will guide you through each stage of the graduate job application process, from identifying what you want to do and what you're good at to understanding how you can convey this in the best way to prospective employers. It includes hints and tips which will give you more confidence to secure the job of your dreams.

How to use this book

You can read it in order, or you can dip in and out of the sections which are most relevant to you. Throughout the book are case studies and stories from graduate recruiters and job hunters. They share examples of what has impressed them as well as what not to do. You'll also find links to many useful tools, such as a CV template and a step-by-step guide to setting up your LinkedIn profile, which will help you promote yourself well to employers.

The book is split into three sections. Part One focuses on the job search and gives you lots of information about the current graduate job market, salaries and application numbers. It will help you understand the market you're entering and plan how you'll navigate your job search. You'll learn how to identify your strengths and values so that you can more easily choose which employers to approach. There are also some activities which will help clarify your thinking and prove useful as you progress through the rest of the book.

If you're already in the job application process and have a clear understanding of it, you might prefer to skip this section and get stuck into Parts Two and Three.

Part Two is all about the job offer. It covers the early stages of the assessment process, from application forms and CVs to online tests and telephone and video interviews. It looks at social media and how this can be used in a positive way during the application process (as well as what to avoid). There's a section focused on the assessment-centre and final-interview stage. This might be your first direct contact with the employer, and it's your opportunity to stand out. You'll learn how to prepare, what to expect and how to perform at your best.

Part Three is about impressing in your job. I'll help you get off on the right foot with employers by advising you how to manage offers if you receive more than one and how to impress from day one. The tools and techniques in this section will enable you to create a great first impression and progress more quickly within your job. Understanding this section will give you an advantage throughout your working life, as the information can be applied throughout your long and successful career.

PART ONE
FINDING A JOB

'If you find a job you love, you will never
have to work again.'
— Anonymous

One
The Graduate Labour Market

Go to university, get a decent degree, apply for a couple of jobs and start the job of your dreams, which is in your ideal location, with a highly regarded employer and a great salary. Is that your plan? Easier said than done.

The reality is that many factors are involved in securing your first job after university. An understanding of the market is a starting point. This information will set you off on the right road. There's a lot of data out there, and if you look at it all, you'll find inconsistencies and contradictions that could leave you feeling more confused than when you started.

At the time of writing, I looked at some graduate recruitment statistics from trusted sources. Some of the statistics are fairly consistent – for example, average salary and sector popularity are two key areas offering a degree of stability.

So, let's start with the basics. What are you up against?

In 2018, 138 employer members of the ISE completed a survey showing 17,667 graduate vacancies for that year. This number has varied between a low of 11,012, in 2003, and a high of 24,126, in 2015.[3] Although these figures represent only a limited number of graduate employers, they clearly show how volatile the market can be. And this is before Brexit.

According to the Employer Skills Survey 2017[4] (conducted by IFF Research, provided by the Department for Education and analysed by HECSU), these were the graduate jobs with the highest numbers of reported vacancies:

- Nurses

- Human resources and industrial relations

- Business sales executives

- Welfare and housing associate professionals

---

3   Hooley, T (2018) *ISE Annual Student Recruitment Survey 2018*.
     https://ise.org.uk/page/ISEPublications, p17.
4   Department for Education (2018) *Employer Skills Survey 2017*.
     https://assets.publishing.service.gov.uk/government/uploads/
     system/uploads/attachment_data/file/746493/ESS_2017_UK_
     Report_Controlled_v06.00.pdf

- IT user support technicians

- Marketing associate professionals

- Programmers and software development professionals

- Engineering professionals

- Sales accounts and business development managers

- Managers and directors in retail and wholesale

- Medical practitioners

- Solicitors

- Vocational and industrial trainers and instructors

- Primary and nursery education teaching professionals

- Business and related associate professionals

- Youth and community workers

- Chartered and certified accountants

In 2019, High Fliers Research also found the biggest growth in graduate vacancies to be in public sector organisations, accounting, professional services firms and engineering and industrial companies.[5]

---

5   High Fliers Research Limited (2019) *The Graduate Market in 2019*. www. highfliers.co.uk/download/2019/graduate_market/GMReport19.pdf

So how many graduates are you competing against? 329,325 first degrees were awarded to UK-domiciled graduates in 2017 and of these graduates, 73.9% were known to be in professional-level jobs six months after graduating.[6]

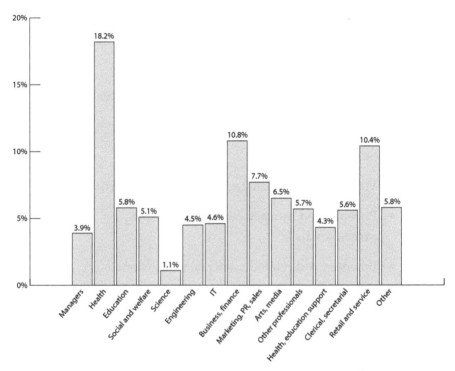

Types of work of 2017 graduates after six months, HECSU, 2019[7]

6   Prospects and the AGCAS Education Liaison Task Group (2019) *What Do Graduates Do 2018/19?* https://luminate.prospects.ac.uk/media/0d64ccf2-aeb9-488e-b77e-fccffa21ec92/what-do-graduates-do-2018-19.pdf, p8.
7   Prospects and AGCAS (2019) *What Do Graduates Do 2018/19?*, p11.

Let's talk money

In the ISE Annual Student Recruitment Survey 2018, employers reported a median graduate starting salary of £28,000. Broken down into sector specifics, it looks like this:

- Finance and professional services = £28,000
- Energy, engineering and industry = £27,500
- Legal = £40,000
- IT = £30,000
- Retail and FMCG = £28,500
- Charity and public sector = £23,056
- Other = £22,000[8]

You may have heard of *The Times Top 100 Graduate Employers*. As the title suggests, it's a book that lists the top 100 employers as voted for by the students taking part in research by High Fliers. According to this book, graduate starting salaries at the UK's leading graduate employers are unchanged for the fifth consecutive year in 2019, at a median starting salary of £30,000.[9]

Bear in mind that ISE members and *Times Top 100* employers are predominantly large employers with

---

8   Hooley (2018) *ISE Annual Student Recruitment Survey 2018*, p40.
9   High Fliers Research Limited (2019) *The Graduate Market in 2019*.

significant graduate schemes. They are more likely to pay at the higher end of the scale. If we look at the Destinations of Leavers from Higher Education (DLHE) survey figures from 2016–2017, median salaries of UK-domiciled full-time leavers who obtained first-degree qualifications and entered full-time paid work in the UK were £24,000 for male professionals and £22,000 for females.[10]

When looking at the highest-paying graduate employers, you'll find some starting salaries in excess of £40,000. If you're motivated by money, then this may entice you to apply. I would advise making use of websites such as Glassdoor to try to understand what it might be like to work for one of these high-paying employers. I once hired a graduate who lasted a year on a highly paid graduate scheme with a budget supermarket retailer. He confirmed rumours that these graduates often slept in the office and rarely took any holiday – a very poor experience. He had been the last one left of his cohort. His colleagues had dropped off at various points throughout year one.

So, salaries are not the be-all and end-all. Your first salary is a 'starting' salary, and many factors will affect how quickly your salary increases. There are other benefits you should consider. Look at the job package as a whole – location, training, progression opportunities,

---

10   HESA (2018) *Higher Education Leavers Statistics: UK, 2016/17 – Salary and location of leavers in employment.* www.hesa.ac.uk/news/28-06-2018/sfr250-higher-education-leaver-statistics-employment

likely job satisfaction, pension, holiday entitlement and other perks. My graduate starting salary was £13,000, which was probably a little below average in 2001. I remember being jealous of friends who had made £17,000, but I'm glad I wasn't blinded by the cash. I had pay rises at least once, sometimes twice, each year in that job. And whenever I was promoted, I also secured a pay increase. Key things happened in my career that positively impacted on pay, and this trajectory wasn't in my mind when I accepted that £13,000 offer.

It's a numbers game

According to the ISE, 69% of graduate recruitment campaigns run from October to December, and 81% of job offers are made by Easter. Getting hired is a competitive game – employer respondents report that they get an average of forty-one applications for every graduate job.[11] This is broken down into sectors in the table overleaf.

EXPERT INSIGHT
M&S typically receives approximately 150 to 220 applications per vacancy, according to Helen, while Ashley at Enterprise Rent-A-Car has more vacancies, with about twenty-three applications per hire.

---

11   Hooley (2018) *ISE Annual Student Recruitment Survey 2018*, p23.

Average number of applications per vacancy by sector, ISE Annual Recruitment Survey 2018 (based on responses from 138 employers covering 17,667 graduate hires)[12]

Sector	Applications per graduate vacancy
FMCG	204
Investment bank or fund managers	86
Energy, water or utilities	86
Banking or financial services	79
Digital	67
Consulting or business services	53
Retail	49
Transport or logistics	46
Engineering or industrial	38
IT and telecommunications	36
Built environment	35
Accountancy or professional services	29
Chemical or pharmaceuticals	29
Law firm	22
Public sector	12

Although application numbers can appear overwhelming and you might ask yourself if there's any point, it's not all bad news. The latest assessment of vacancies by *The Times Top 100 Graduate Employers* confirms that employers are expecting to step up their graduate recruitment by an impressive 9.1% in

---

12 Hooley (2018) *ISE Annual Student Recruitment Survey 2018*, p29.

2019, the highest annual rise in vacancies for university-leavers for nine years. In addition to that, 20,420 graduates actually started work with the organisations featured in *The Times Top 100 Graduate Employers* in 2018, but more than 700 graduate roles were left unfilled due to insufficient applications[13]. Therefore, some schemes are still undersubscribed.

MY TOP TIP

Be mindful of advertised application deadline dates as some employers will close early if they fill positions as they go. Applying early will increase your chances of success.

A graduate scheme vs a graduate job

Are you applying for a graduate scheme or a graduate job? There are some subtle differences between the two options. Let's look at the key characteristics of each.

Graduate scheme:

- Usually offered by large, successful and well-known businesses (you'd likely be working in a corporate environment)

- Highly competitive with limited places – only 14% of applicants are successful[14]

---

13 High Fliers Research Limited (2019) *The Graduate Market in 2019*.
14 Usher, S (2013) 'No Grad Scheme, No Worries', *The Independent*, 1 August.

- Often involves multiple application stages over a long period of time

- Usually provides structured training and support over a set period of time (one to three years), possibly through classroom learning and a mentor

- Offers more opportunities for personal development, usually within different areas of the business

- A job or a promotion is not necessarily guaranteed at the end of it

Graduate job:

- Requires high-calibre graduates but may be open only to those who have already graduated

- Training and career progression is likely to be less structured (more flexible arrangement)

- More likely to be offered by an SME (small to medium-sized enterprise), where you could have more practical experience, increased responsibility and a greater impact on the business's success

There are pros and cons to both, depending on what's important to you. If you value job security and are looking at graduate schemes, you might apply only for those which guarantee a job at the end. Graduate schemes can be perceived as more prestigious, and indeed, they're usually offered by well-known employers and tend to provide higher salaries. Their structured training can give you a great start in your career. But this route could make you feel as if you're one of many. The training can feel impersonal.

The SME job market is currently experiencing a boom, with the rise of tech company growth in particular. SMEs account for 99.9% of all private sector business in the UK and are where most graduates work. But many new graduates are unaware of the graduate jobs they offer. While smaller companies are unlikely to offer a long and structured training programme, they're likely to provide rich on-the-job training and opportunities to stand out as one of a smaller number of graduates – you may even be the only one.

Strategies on how to impress in whichever role you secure are included in Part Three of this book. For now, I want you to get clear on whom you plan to apply to.

Two
Finding Your Strengths

We all have our strengths and weaknesses, and a job that plays to your strengths is likely to be more fun. By figuring out your strengths early and factoring them into your job search, you're more likely to be successful at the job you land – and you're more likely to love that job.

Understanding your strengths

Some sectors may value certain skills above others. Broadly speaking though, most employers are looking for similar skills from their graduate recruits. Bear in mind that they may not be looking for a huge number of technical skills at this point because these can be taught at a later stage. During recruitment, they're looking for you to be motivated and enthusiastic about the opportunity and are more likely to be assessing you on soft skills, such as communication and teamwork.

Take a look at the table opposite, which highlights the skills employers find graduates to be lacking.

Concern about resilience was most commonly cited in terms of graduates. Interestingly, school leavers are considered to be more resilient than graduates.

You can use this table to get an understanding of the skills that employers are looking for. Consider which of these are your strengths and which are your development areas. Can you think of examples from university life (ideally outside of your course) or work experience which best illustrate a particular strength?

TASK: Identify your strengths and weaknesses

- Write down your strengths
- Write down your weaknesses
- Ask a friend or family member to write down what they think your strengths and weaknesses are
- Compare the lists, discussing any points of interest with your friend or family member
- Identify your top three strengths and come up with examples of where you have demonstrated these
- Identify your top three weaknesses and come up with ideas on how you could develop these

---

Proportion of employers who say entry-level hires lack particular skills, ISE Student Development Survey 2019[15]

	Graduates	Apprentices	School leavers
Resilience	67%	67%	55%
Managing up	65%	69%	70%
Leadership	64%	68%	70%
Commercial awareness	61%	79%	80%
Dealing with conflict	59%	67%	70%
Self-awareness	59%	55%	60%
Career management	55%	62%	60%
Job-specific technical skills	54%	75%	85%
Negotiation/influencing skills	49%	62%	65%
Emotional intelligence	47%	55%	50%
Business appropriate communication	46%	76%	80%
Time management	32%	52%	45%
Taking responsibility	31%	43%	35%
Listening	26%	37%	20%
Presentation skills	24%	61%	65%
Data handling/data analysis	21%	52%	50%
Problem-solving	21%	39%	35%
Excel skills	18%	29%	40%
Interpersonal skills	17%	38%	30%
Staying positive	16%	23%	20%
Writing	14%	30%	25%
Teamwork	11%	20%	15%
Dressing appropriately	9%	36%	20%
IT/digital skills	8%	20%	20%
Numeracy	6%	10%	15%

15   Hooley, T (2019) *ISE Student Development Survey 2019*. https://ise.org.uk/page/ISEPublications, p16.

EXPERT INSIGHT

'Get involved in lots of different activities while you're at university. Join a couple of clubs or societies, be active in the student union, play sports, do some voluntary work, get yourself a mentor if you can. Along with your studies and any part-time jobs, these activities will expose you to lots of different situations and give you opportunities to try new things, and you'll find out what you enjoy (and what you don't enjoy) and what you're good at. As well as helping you to understand your preferences and strengths, getting involved in lots of activities will help you build up plenty of examples for your applications and interviews.' (Gary)

The importance of work experience

Over a third of recruiters who took part in the High Fliers 2019 research repeated their warnings from previous years: graduates who have no previous work experience are unlikely to be successful during the selection.[16] This is backed up by Helen, Head of Future Talent Recruitment. Reflecting on her time at M&S, she says, 'Work experience is key. It doesn't necessarily have to be directly relevant, although this varies by scheme – for example, to become a fashion designer or buyer, it would be more useful to have relevant work experience. It definitely gives candidates more

---

16   High Fliers Research Limited (2019) *The Graduate Market in 2019.* www.highfliers.co.uk/download/2019/graduate_market/ GMReport19.pdf

to draw upon at interview and assessment, more confidence and the ability to better transition into the world of work.'

Some of the best work experience comes in the form of an internship or placement with an employer you're considering for a graduate role. This can be a great way to find out if the employer is a good fit for you. You might end up hating the work, but you will have been paid for the experience, can discard the employer from your future job searches and can enjoy the benefit of having the experience on your CV. The best-case scenario is you enjoy the placement, they love you and you head back to your final year at university with a graduate job offer in hand. Indeed, ISE employers reported that they rehired an average of 52% of their interns and 43% of their summer placement students.[17]

MY TOP TIP

Application numbers for placements and internships tend to be much lower than for graduate jobs, so I definitely recommend trying to secure one.

My view is that work experience is a key way to differentiate yourself from the competition. There's a benchmark on qualifications for graduate roles, so you might have to have a 2:1 and a certain number

---

17   Hooley, T (2018) *ISE Annual Student Recruitment Survey 2018.* https://ise.org.uk/page/ISEPublications, p9.

of UCAS points to even apply. Because so many applicants will meet this standard, work experience can be the way to stand out. It's certainly an advantage to have work experience that's relevant to the role, whether you were paid for the work or not, but don't discount the value of a part-time or summer job that seems unconnected to what you want to do.

EXPERT INSIGHT

'Work experience is great because it gives you tangible examples to talk about, and as a recruiter I love examples: they show me that you can actually do all the things you talk about on your CV. It's great if the work experience is in a relevant area – that is the "gold standard" if you like – but work experience in other areas is valuable too. Recruiters look for transferable skills: something you have learned in one context but could use somewhere else. For example, a project you've undertaken while volunteering in your local community can teach you about planning, teamwork, resilience, leadership – a whole range of skills that you'll be using in your graduate job. Tell me about what you've learned in one situation and show me how you'll transfer those skills to my organisation and you'll definitely catch my attention.' (Gary)

STUDENT CASE STUDY: JOSH, UNIVERSITY OF LEEDS

Josh was looking for a graduate role in management consulting. He had a passion for this type of work, but he felt his work experience to date wasn't relevant to his ambition. This resulted in him falling back on university course examples at interview. We discussed how course examples could be used by all the applicants but that work experience examples tend to be more unique. On reflection, Josh was able to identify skills from his role working in a gym – teamwork, working under pressure, coaching, etc – that were transferable to any workplace.

But what if you have no work experience? I coached a graduate a couple of years ago who had an outstanding academic track record. Sarah had the highest marks in her GCSEs and A-levels, as well as the top grades in her undergraduate and master's degrees. She was ready to get her first graduate job but couldn't get beyond the application form stage. We quickly identified that this was due to her lack of work experience and inability to make her responses unique or impressive. Sarah did have some voluntary work experience which she hadn't shared on her applications. As it was unpaid, she didn't think it was relevant. She had also taken part in some interesting activities in university. When we looked more closely at these, it was easy to identify some examples which showcased her transferable skills and provided much stronger answers for her applications. This was a light-bulb moment for Sarah – 'I really believe that the advice I was given was directly related to me eventually finding a job, and not just any job, but one which was exactly what I wanted.'

EXPERT INSIGHT

'Work experience helps you gain exposure to situations and working environments that you may never have considered as potential career options. It will also help you to understand more about what you enjoy, what you don't, and what would really excite you and get you out of bed in the morning as a potential career. I don't think it has to be relevant as long as you're able to reflect and articulate how the skills and experiences you have are transferable and relevant to other roles. If you want to work in a competitive area or profession – ie law, accounting – then some relevant experience and/or showing a real passion for the area (eg through reading journals or industry magazines, etc) would be an advantage.' (Tonia)

Extracurricular activities

Most students get involved in activities at university (or outside of university) which aren't directly related to their course. This can be a great way to make friends and do what you love. It also provides a wealth of opportunities to add interesting and transferable skills to your CV and application which you can then talk about at interview.

Look out for opportunities to take on responsibility within these activities. Can you be in charge of increasing membership numbers – a great example of influencing and sales? Or can you work your way up to a leadership role? Sports clubs provide great opportunities for teamwork and leadership. Being a course rep would highlight communication skills and perhaps an ability to deal with conflict. When you start to think of your hobbies in this way, it's easy to find transferable skills.

EXPERT INSIGHT

'Society leadership positions, student rep or course rep are useful responsibilities to take on at university. Don't undersell or rule out anything done in addition to your degree course.' (Ashley)

Don't restrict your activities to only what's available. If a club or society doesn't exist, create your own! This would be a great way to demonstrate innovation, influence employers (perhaps to secure sponsorship) and lead a team. Or you might have a side hustle going on outside of university – even better if it's something with a tangible output (a store on eBay that makes you £500 a month, for example).

EXPERT INSIGHT

'Some of the most impressive examples tend to relate to specific ventures that the student has created and driven – those with real entrepreneurial flare. In M&S we had an applicant for our Food Product Development scheme who had established his own ice cream brand and mobile selling. It doesn't have to be that grand though – the Duke of Edinburgh's Award is still a great thing to have on your CV, as are volunteering opportunities and charity initiatives. The key is to be able to articulate what skills and experiences they have provided, what you've learned from them and how that's translatable into the world of work.' (Helen)

Making the best use of your time at university will help you secure a graduate role. You need to achieve a balance between developing strong technical skills in your degree and soft skills that make you more employable. With Teaching Excellence and Student Outcomes Framework (TEF) and Graduate Outcomes, universities are under a lot more pressure to show how they're developing students' employability. Careers services are often underutilised, so investigate what support they can offer, whether through employability workshops, career consultants, employer contacts or alumni networks.

MY TOP TIP

Some universities have created innovative and even revolutionary programmes that make candidates more attractive to different industries. Visit your careers service and see how they can help you.

Getting clear on your career plan

It's vital to have a clear career strategy. It will help you manage the direction you want your career to take, as well as identify and acquire the skills, qualities and experiences you'll need.

How you go about identifying your career strategy is up to you. Some people may take a detailed approach whereas others may be more visual and use only key points to focus their direction – either way, it needs to work for you. Take time to think before ploughing into applications and job searches.

Are you clear on the skills, qualities and knowledge you have? Once you know these things, you can match them to the job roles you're interested in. You'll also be aware of any areas that you may need to develop to achieve your career goals.

- What skills and qualities do I have?
- What am I good at?
- What do I need to develop?
- What are the requirements for the job I want to secure?
- What are my own job requirements?

Being able to answer these questions will allow you to really sell yourself at interview and enable you to showcase what you can bring to the job and the organisation.

To get started, visit www.sophiemilliken.co.uk/from-learner-to-earner-resources to download an early career plan.

MY TOP TIP

Be realistic about the skills and knowledge you have. If you don't have certain skills, there's no point lying about them, as you're likely to be caught out. Consider what you bring and focus on your strengths.

Career options

Figuring out which job roles will suit you best and how to apply your skills and qualities can be the most difficult part of setting your career plan. Think of your options and review them against your values and preferences, considering these questions:

- Which job roles best suit my skill set?

- What areas could I see myself working in?

More information on researching job roles and organisations can be found later in Chapter Three.

What if you don't know what to do?

EXPERT INSIGHT

'Visit your university careers service. The careers advisors will be able to help you think through your career options and might suggest ideas that you've not thought of before – eg by sharing information showing what other students who studied your course did after they graduated or putting you in touch with alumni.

Remember, you don't have to know what you want to do before you make an appointment: careers advisors do their jobs because they genuinely enjoy the process of helping students work through their options, and they will be very happy to help you.' (Gary)

It's time to start making some decisions. Think about the information you've gathered and start to formulate what your career goals might look like over the next few years. The SMARTER model can help you break down your goals. SMARTER goals are specific, measurable, achievable, realistic, timely, exciting and reviewable.

Specific: Be as clear as you can and avoid ambiguous statements.

Measurable: You need to be able to see what you've achieved.

Achievable: Your goal should motivate you but be attainable.

Realistic: It should be reasonable and avoid the realm of fantasy.

Timely: Create time frames for completing steps towards the goal (for example, doing short courses or talking with someone about the skills required for a particular job).

Exciting: The goal should be something you actually want, so you'll be motivated during the time it takes to achieve it.

Reviewable: Don't set your goal in concrete; be flexible.

Visit www.sophiemilliken.co.uk/from-learner-to-earner-resources to download a goal-setting worksheet.

This career-planning checklist might be a useful tool to get you thinking about the preparation you need to do before starting your job search.

Career-planning checklist

- Do you need additional job skills, experience or information?
- What areas of yourself will you need to develop?
- Do you need to develop a wider network or links with specific people?
- Is there additional training you need to do (perhaps to gain specific qualifications or skills)?
- Do you need to find ways to demonstrate your skills and knowledge so you can provide evidence of what you can do?
- What kind of work experience would be helpful to you?

- Are there any changes you could make to the way you deal with people or work situations that might increase your likelihood of achieving your goals? How will you start to do this?

- With whom can you discuss your goals? When will you do this?

- Are you clear about the type of work you'd like to do? How can you clarify this further?

- Do you have a supportive network? Do you believe you're recognised as able to contribute information to this network? If not, what could you do about this?

- Do you have a mentor with whom you can discuss both the technical content and the intangibles of your job? If not, have you thought about finding a mentor? Is there someone in your workplace or elsewhere you could approach?

- Do you need to make radical changes to your present direction? What are the first steps to achieving this change in direction and how will you take these steps?

- Do you think you'll need to undertake further study? What steps could you take to do this?

- Do you feel in charge of your career direction? If not, how can you gain confidence and take charge?

Your values/company values

Employers will often encourage their employees to complete engagement surveys, so they can identify the most important characteristics in the employment relationship. They want to know how to keep their employees motivated. You can use the same characteristics to identify what you're looking for from your dream employer when carrying out your job search.

Here are some characteristics for you to consider.

Culture and work environment

While remuneration packages and company benefits may appeal to lots of potential candidates, the organisation's culture is often what determines whether an employee will fit and actually enjoy the job. The working environment will also determine if an employee will be happy in the workplace. Ask yourself:

- Does the culture fit with my personal values and principles?

- Does the organisation provide a healthy, positive and encouraging working environment?

- Does the organisation celebrate success and recognise people's achievements?

Flexibility

Another important factor is work-life balance. You shouldn't be expected to always work long hours at the expense of your personal life. Employers should consider reasonable time off for employees, including holidays, paternity and maternity leave. Many employers offer flexible working arrangements such as working-at-home days or time banking to help employees get the right balance.

Consider how you can get the right work-life balance:

- What would work for you if you had the choice?

- What is the organisation's approach to flexible working?

- What policies does the organisation already have in place?

A great example of an employer offering flexibility is brand licensing company The Point.1888. On their website, their values are exceptionally clear. And their blog on what they call 'lifework balance' highlights examples of their flexible working approach.[18]

---

18 The Point.1888 (2019) 'Lifework Balance: Flexible working for all'. https://thepoint1888.com/flexible-working-for-all

Involvement

Working for an organisation shouldn't just be about doing the role and getting paid at the end of the month. You should feel as if you're part of the organisation, have the ability to influence, and can suggest new ideas.

- Does the organisation welcome new ideas?
- Do they welcome feedback and accept suggestions on how they can develop?
- Do they give employees autonomy to make decisions?
- Do they allow employees to take ownership for work or projects?

Opportunities to develop your career

Your future employer should take personal and career development seriously. Investing in these things ensures people continue to have the skills and abilities necessary to perform in ever-changing job roles. It's also an opportunity to grow talent within the organisation.

When researching, ask yourself:

- Does the organisation have the right paths to allow me to develop my career?

- What are the opportunities to train and gain new experience?

- How have other people in the organisation progressed?

- What is the typical career path in the job I'm applying for?

Self-awareness

You need to consider what's important to you, as we all have different values and motivations.

Ask yourself these three simple questions:

- What is important to me?

- What are my values?

- What motivates me?

The answers to these questions will help you work out what you need to be happy and motivated in your new job.

As well as competencies, employers are putting more emphasis on values, but it can be difficult to work out what your values actually are. It might feel much easier to simply list skills and then try to manipulate these into values. But skills and values are different things. Values are lasting beliefs or ideals about what's good or bad and desirable or undesirable.

They have a major influence on a person's behaviour and attitude. You can find a list of organisational values with a little bit of digging on an employer's website. If you can't find them, you could always get in touch to ask if they have a document they're willing to share with you.

But before looking at the organisation's values, establish your own – then you can make a comparison. You can find lots of online exercises to help you identify your values, but try this quick one to get you started.

TASK: Identify your values

The following list of values will help you develop a clearer sense of what's most important to you in life. Simply copy or print this list, mark the values which resonate with you most and then sort them in order of priority.

While some values will have little or no significance to you (they may even seem negative), others will call to you, and you'll think, 'Yes, this value is a part of me.'

Use this values list as a guide. It's not exhaustive, so feel free to add others. I recommend selecting no more than five core values to focus on because if everything is a core value, then nothing is a priority.

Achievement	Fame	Peace
Adventure	Friendships	Pleasure
Authenticity	Fun	Poise
Authority	Growth	Popularity
Autonomy	Happiness	Recognition
Balance	Honesty	Religion
Beauty	Humour	Reputation
Boldness	Influence	Respect
Challenge	Inner Harmony	Responsibility
Citizenship	Justice	Security
Community	Kindness	Self-Respect
Compassion	Knowledge	Service
Competency	Leadership	Spirituality
Contribution	Learning	Stability
Creativity	Love	Status
Curiosity	Loyalty	Success
Determination	Meaningful Work	Trustworthiness
Fairness	Openness	Wealth
Faith	Optimism	Wisdom

Now that you have a clearer understanding of which values matter to you, you can identify your best employer match based on what they stand for. You should also find it easier to answer application-form and interview questions. You might even spot the ones which are linked to values and be able to provide examples of when you have demonstrated them.

MY TOP TIP

Try to get into the workplaces which interest you to see if the employers actually practise the values they claim to have. Do this by following up on any contacts you have, attending insight days or through your careers service.

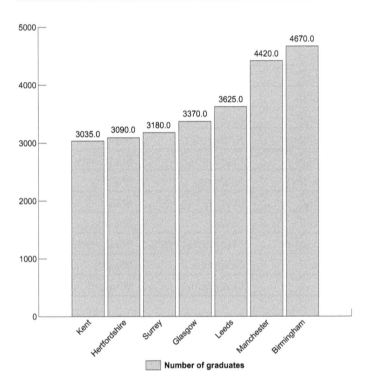

Number of graduates

Top locations for graduate employment outside London, Prospects Luminate 2018[19]

19 Prospects and the AGCAS Education Liaison Task Group (2019) *What Do Graduates Do 2018/19?* https://luminate.prospects.ac.uk/media/0d64ccf2-aeb9-488e-b77e-fccffa21ec92/what-do-graduates-do-2018-19.pdf, p10.

Location, location, location

According to 'Graduate labour market 2018' from Prospects Luminate, the market is becoming more urban. The proportion of graduates starting their career in London increased to 22.4% of all graduates.

In their Annual Recruitment Survey 2018, the ISE confirmed that their employer respondents recruited 39% of their graduates into London, with the next highest being 9% in the south-east.[20]

There is increasing pressure on employers to diversify their workforce with regards to location, but statistics confirm that graduates still prefer to pursue jobs near their home or university. You need to think about whether location is important to you. Some employers will ask if you're mobile. Not showing flexibility on this can sometimes result in being rejected at an early stage. Don't be tempted to say you're fully mobile if you aren't, as this will cause problems for you and the employer further along in the recruitment process. Instead, make sure you're clear on where the locations are and how much say you have in where you would be placed.

---

20   Hooley (2018) *ISE Annual Student Recruitment Survey 2018*, p43.

STUDENT CASE STUDY: CHLOE, UNIVERSITY OF MANCHESTER

Chloe wanted to be based in London and saw her future in the capital long-term. But she ticked the box to say she was fully mobile on her application to John Lewis. She performed well during the assessment process and was offered the job in Newcastle and then Aberdeen. Chloe decided to embrace the opportunity to live in two new cities. She knew this was short-term and didn't have any ties at this early stage in her career. She contacted the other graduates who were given these locations and they flat-shared, saving money and developing a great bond. Chloe stayed flexible with her location for about three years, taking chances to gain promotions with each move she made. She eventually reached a point where she focused on getting back to London with the confidence of being in a senior manager role. After a few months of waiting for the right opportunity, she achieved this and has remained in London since then.

MY TOP TIP

Showing flexibility in terms of location early on in your career can give you opportunities to progress that those more fixed on one location will miss. Be open to new and exciting experiences that you can make the most of before you reach a point in your life where you might be keener to settle down and have ties to one area. Be as flexible as you can be for as long as you can be.

Three
The Job Search

Starting your career search is exciting but can also be daunting if you don't know where to start.

EXPERT INSIGHT

'Try and get as much experience of different things as possible so that you get a feel for what you really enjoy – don't be afraid to try different things. Think about the different types of sectors and opportunities within them and do some research, watch some videos and network.' (Tonia)

Before you spend time submitting an application form, sending over a CV and cover letter or attending an interview, it's important to research the organisation you want to work for.

Research the organisation

An organisation's website is the first place to start your research. Here, you'll often find information on key markets, clients, products and services as well as financial or strategic reports and mission statements. You may be able to see customer feedback, understand more about the organisation's values and determine whether you feel the culture fits with your own values and aims.

Take note of key information such as the aims of the company, their annual turnover and number of employees, their organisational structure, their key competitors and their position in the industry. Knowing this will help you show the employer why you're the best fit. It will show them that you're knowledgeable and generally interested in who the company is and what they do.

MY TOP TIPS

- Analyse the sector or industry
- Use your careers service
- Check out social media profiles (I explore this in more detail later in this chapter)
- Meet the employer at events
- Visit working environments if possible – it's a great way to get a feel for an organisation directly
- Speak to friends and family

EXPERT INSIGHT

'Remember that your careers service isn't just there to check your CV or arrange job fairs: the team will include experienced professionals who have a broad view of the labour market and can help you plan ahead. Visit them as soon as you can – ideally in your first year, when you have more time to act on their advice. And even if you're already nearing the end of your studies, many universities continue to offer careers support to students after they've graduated. It's an excellent (and free!) resource, so make the most of it.' (Gary)

Research the job

Most organisations will send you a job description or person specification as part of the application process, but it's useful to research a little further.

- How does the role fit with other roles within the organisation?

- Who are the key stakeholders you'll be working with?

- What line management or reporting responsibilities will the role involve?

- What level of autonomy or supervision will you have?

- What are the opportunities to train and develop your skills further?

Speak their language

Each organisation has its own distinct language, values and core competencies. These things underpin the culture.

When researching, note any words that stand out. Pay attention to those that relate to skills, qualities or behaviours – that way, you can use similar language in your application or during an interview.

Career fairs and how to conduct yourself

Career fairs are great places to speak face-to-face with recruiters and hiring managers and learn about current vacancies or potential opportunities. They're also fantastic places to network and develop your connections, which will help you take your career that one step further. You may get to meet some current graduates. This is a brilliant opportunity to ask them honest questions about their experiences with the employer. You also might have the chance to impress a recruiter who can fast-track you through the process, or at least help you enhance your application. If you progress through the application process, it's likely you'll meet this recruiter again, so be memorable for the right reasons.

EXPERT INSIGHT
'I can still tell you the name of the person who has created the biggest impact on me at a grad fair – so

much so I can tell you the date, location, and what she's doing now as we've kept in touch via the wonders of LinkedIn. She didn't do anything wacky – she did the basics but did them exceptionally well. She'd done her homework on the company, the scheme, the role. She'd prepped questions to ask (and much more focused than the typical "what do you do?" ones) – and the questions were in line with the company, ie we were a commercial and people-focused business, and thus her questions were commercially and people centric. She confidently approached the stand. She introduced herself, said she was interested, wanted to know more, and generally did a really impressive job selling herself without "shouting" about it. She left us with a CV and with a firm plan around what we would do next to take her interest forward.' (David)

Here are some tips to help you get the most out of the careers-fair experience.

Be clear on why you're attending

Whether you're currently looking for a job or not, career fairs have lots of benefits. It's important to know why you're attending, or at the very least which employers you'd like to speak to, otherwise you're likely to waste your time. Maybe you want to find out more about an organisation or learn what job opportunities might be available. Maybe you want some advice on applications or writing your CV. Whatever it is, know the purpose and leave feeling like you've achieved it.

Carry out your research

Never underestimate the power of preparation and research. Careers-fair websites will have lots of detailed information about the event: attendees, guest speakers, workshops, etc. A good place to start is to find out which organisations are attending.

You may want to explore the current or potential job vacancies or do more research into the organisation's culture and what makes them an attractive employer. Doing this will help you think of questions you might wish to ask.

Prepare your elevator pitch: Who are you? What makes you interesting? Why would an employer want to employ you? Be prepared to have conversations with these employers. Be curious and show interest in what they're offering.

Dress appropriately

Making a good first impression and looking professional should always be your main priority. Think of career fairs as somewhere between a job interview and a work event. See this as an opportunity to sell yourself to potential employers. Why would they take you seriously when you're dressed in jogging bottoms and trainers? You can't go wrong with smart shirts, trousers, skirts or dresses and appropriate footwear. Look smart and professional to stand out from the crowd.

Remember, the people you speak to could have real influence in the recruitment process and have good relationships with the hiring managers.

Network and make connections

Networking is an extremely powerful tool. Knowing more people gives you greater access, facilitates the sharing of information and makes it easier to influence others. It's far easier to influence people you know than it is to influence strangers. Reach out, chat and be curious about who people are and the organisations they represent.

There's a trend towards virtual (online) career fairs. The downside is you won't get to meet the employer in person, but they could still broaden your access. You may also find that few students take advantage of this opportunity, leading to a more valuable experience for you.

Follow up your conversations

Be sure to follow up the conversations you had and connections you made a few days later. You might consider emailing people directly to thank them for their time, or connecting with them via LinkedIn.

Be the one to stand out and leave a lasting impression.

Here are some examples to get you started.

Hi <<their name>>,

It was great chatting with you earlier today at the <<event name here>>.

I am <<details about how they might remember you or context about you>>. I wanted to thank you for explaining more about you and the positions available at <<company name>>. After speaking with you, I got really excited about a future at <<company name>>.

It would be great to connect with you on LinkedIn.

Kind regards

<<Your Name>>

Useful follow-up email message

Hi <<their name>>,

It was great chatting with you earlier today at the <<event name here>>.

I am <<details about how they might remember you or context about you>>. I wanted to thank you for explaining more about you and the positions available at <<company name>>. After speaking with you, I got really excited about a future at <<company name>>.

Please let me know if there is anything else you need from me.

I attach my CV for reference.

Kind regards

<<Your Name>>
<<Your signature including LinkedIn URL>>
<<ATTACH YOUR CV TAILORED TO THIS COMPANY>>

STUDENT CASE STUDY: LIZZIE, UNIVERSITY OF MANCHESTER

I met Lizzie at a careers fair in Manchester. She was super keen and came prepared to ask me some specific questions about the John Lewis scheme. She was smart and well prepared and came across as unbelievably enthusiastic. I spent about half an hour chatting to her and also spotted her in the front row of a talk I gave at the event. She asked for my business card and used this to follow up with me professionally a few days later. She impressed me enormously at this stage.

EXPERT INSIGHT

'It might sound obvious, but students who had done some research into our company before the event always impressed me. That's partly because it was so rare: 95% of students approached me with the same, obvious questions. That's fine in one sense: campus events are there for you to gather information from employers after all. But a student who had already taken the time to understand what our company did and the market we operated in, and instead used the conversation to ask more probing questions about our graduate scheme or the qualities that our most successful employees demonstrated always stood out for me. I often remembered them several months later when I met them at assessment centres.' (Gary)

Other tips to consider

- Ensure you know why you're attending and for what purpose

- Do your research (both on the event and the employers)

- Know which key employers you'd like to speak with

- Ensure you look professional and dress appropriately

- Have a CV and cover letter prepared to hand out to potential employers

- Enjoy the day, make new connections and start developing your network

Networking

As mentioned, networking is a powerful tool. There are many different ways to get in front of employers you want to meet. A careers fair is an ideal opportunity, as the employers are there specifically to speak to students. But you can also make use of the events being run by your careers service. Employers often come on campus to run company presentations or skills sessions. These are excellent opportunities to learn more about the company and are likely to provide time for you to meet one-to-one with the recruiter. Your lecturers might have contacts at some of the organisations which interest you, so talk to them if possible. You might also have friends or family who can make an introduction. Be creative in finding ways to meet with employers that interest you.

Best practice in contacting employers

Employers tend to have small graduate recruitment teams. With so many universities in the UK, it's not possible for them to have a presence on every campus. On average, employers visit twenty universities.[21] It used to be that employers would use the league tables to select the universities they engaged with and would mostly visit those perceived as 'the best'. Often, senior leaders in a business would influence university choice, and recruitment teams would be encouraged to go to Durham or the London School of Economics (LSE) because the CEO and most of his leadership team had once been students there. I'm pleased to say that thinking has moved on in recent years and employers are encouraged to visit a wider range of universities, driven in particular by the diversity agenda and the push to improve social mobility within their hires.

If your preferred employers are present on your campus, make the most of opportunities to meet and engage with them. Always ask sensible and good questions and don't miss the chance to start building a relationship. Don't let the fact that they're at your campus make you complacent, though. It's unlikely to give you a huge advantage in terms of being fast-tracked through the process (although this can happen on occasion). You'll still be competing with candidates from all universities.

I recommend exploring how you can connect with SMEs. There has been huge growth in this sector,

---

21   High Fliers Research Limited (2019) *The Graduate Market in 2019.* www.highfliers.co.uk/download/2019/graduate_market/ GMReport19.pdf

and as they tend to have small recruitment teams (if they have them at all), they don't always have the resources to connect with universities or promote themselves as much as the larger corporates. Have a chat with your careers service to see what they advise. Perhaps the careers service runs an event specifically for SME employers, which would be well worth attending. Consider your preferred location, as your university will clearly be focused on local SMEs – you might need to look in a different city. Your careers service may also be able to put you in touch with their equivalent team in your desired location.

EXPERT INSIGHTS

'We visit between fifteen and twenty universities – factors are based on where we historically have good conversions, the right university courses, Trendence research, and we visit a mix of Russell and non-Russell Group universities.' (Helen)

'We are more unusual as we manage to visit about 100 universities due to our large hiring plan and regional recruitment teams.' (Ashley)

'In terms of deciding where to go, we'd love to have high engagement with every university, but we have to make decisions to focus on particular ones based on where we operate geographically (and thus where we can accommodate graduates), where we feel we're likely to be attractive to the university's graduate population, where we're likely to identify talent for our leadership programme, etc.' (David)

If an employer you want to meet isn't planning to come to your campus, try contacting them directly. Your university careers service might even have a contact within that organisation. Here are a few things you can do before getting in touch.

Know what's on your CV

Surprisingly, many candidates don't actually know what's written on their own CVs. You should know your CV off by heart. During initial conversations, you're likely to be asked to share your skills and experiences, so it's important that what you're saying matches what's on your CV. Expect potential employers to ask you questions about specific parts of your CV.

Know your stuff inside out as being hesitant may lead employers to question everything on your CV. If you said you took a gap year to go travelling, know where you went and be prepared to share some interesting facts about what you did.

If you supported your student union as a rep, know what you achieved and how you supported your fellow students. If you secured an internship as part of your university degree, know what you learned and how this has cemented your future career plans. And remember to tailor your CV to each employer.

Be ready for contact

First things first. Before sending off your CV or contacting an employer, make sure you're ready to be contacted. If your email address is still igopartying everynight@internetprovider.com, I recommend you change it to something more suitable and professional. The same applies to your voicemail. You don't want a potential employer to be greeted with an inappropriate or funny message. When you receive a call from an unknown number, answer in a clear and professional manner, with a hello and your name. Don't answer thinking you're speaking to your best mate or an annoying cold caller.

Follow the rules

Whether you're making contact speculatively or responding to a message from a potential employer, there are a few rules to follow. Be sure to read through the recruitment pages of the organisation's website. Often these have answers to a number of initial questions you may have. And knowing these answers will show you've done your research. Recruiters and employers get asked a lot of questions, so make sure your questions are thought through, relevant and likely to engage their interest.

If you're asked to complete an online application, don't just send through your CV. If they ask for a cover letter, be sure to include one. Not following simple instructions can mean instant rejection. Carefully read any instructions and always remain professional.

EXPERT INSIGHT

'Give some consideration to how you make contact with the employer. I will be selective about students that I connect with on social media and am more likely to connect if I have already engaged in a conversation elsewhere rather than if I've received a cold call invite.' (Helen)

Where to find jobs

Job websites remain one of the most powerful tools for new job seekers.

I've pulled together my top fifteen graduate job searching sites to help you focus your search and ensure that you have access to the very best job vacancies.

Here they are, in no particular order.

Prospects.ac.uk/graduate-jobs

Proud winner of Best Specialist Job Board in the 2017 National Online Recruitment Awards, Prospects allows you to search a huge range of graduate jobs, graduate schemes, internships and work experience opportunities.

Gradtouch.com

Gradtouch promote the latest graduate jobs and opportunities in a fun and engaging way. They have some great advice on their website, and having collaborated with the founding directors and Durham University graduates, Zac and Joe, on several occasions, I can confirm that they're great to work with.

Milkround.com/jobs

Milkround has been around for years and advertises a wide range of placement and graduate job opportunities. Start your job search or use the advice pages to research careers and help with your decision-making.

RateMyPlacement.co.uk

RateMyPlacement is another of the UK's leading job resources for undergraduates seeking graduate jobs, graduate schemes, internships and work placements. It was set up by three graduates who wanted to offer students a Trip Advisor review-style way to rate their placements. This continues to be an excellent resource to get a true insight into companies.

Targetjobs.co.uk

Use Targetjobs to search for internships, graduate jobs and schemes, and professional postgraduate courses.

This site provides some great information on each sector, making it a valuable research tool. It is also known for advertising year-round vacancies so you might find some good roles here outside of the traditional application window.

Indeed.co.uk

Indeed is the number one job search site worldwide, with over 200 million unique visitors each month. Although it isn't known for being a graduate job website specifically, it is a worth a look. You will find graduate-level jobs, and SMEs and charities are likely to use this over some of the graduate-specific websites, as it is a cost-effective way to advertise.

Universal Jobmatch – https://findajob.dwp.gov.uk

This is the British Government website for finding both full-time and part-time job vacancies. It's no longer officially known as 'Universal Jobmatch', so I've included the new link above.

Reed.co.uk

Take a look at reed.co.uk and you'll find jobs spanning forty-two industry specialisms across the UK and beyond. You can search by location and there are useful tools such as the salary checker and careers advice.

Totaljobs.com

Totaljobs.com is one of the UK's leading jobs boards, attracting job seekers on the hunt through the 110,000 live job ads the site carries at any one time. All of this activity generates over two million applications a month, cementing Totaljobs.com's strong reputation among job seekers and recruiters alike.

CV-Library.co.uk

CV-Library is another leading independent job site in the UK. Candidates are able to apply directly to over 145,000 live vacancies from across the UK, covering over seventy different sectors. Job seekers can register their CV for free and be headhunted by the UK's top recruiters and direct employers. CV-Library will also send email alerts with jobs that are relevant to your experience.

Jobsite.co.uk

Jobsite is a leading British jobs board and you can search over 150,000 vacancies through its job search tool every month. It provides relevant, personalised opportunities to connect high-quality candidates with some of the UK's most successful businesses and offers a specific search function for internships.

Monster.co.uk

Monster is a world leader when it comes to successfully connecting people with job opportunities. With over five million UK website visitors a month, and thousands of jobs from entry-level to management roles, it is definitely worth a stop on your job search journey.

jobs.nhs.uk

NHS Jobs is a niche jobs board making a surprise appearance in my top fifteen. But with around 25,000 jobs advertised on the website every month and 3.9 million visitors, you can see why it made the cut. If you're looking to begin or develop your career in the NHS, this site should be your first port of call.

Fish4.co.uk

Fish4Jobs is visited by over 1.6 million job seekers a month. It is featured in the recruitment section of the *Daily Mirror* and 100+ regional newspapers. Its search function allows you to focus your hunt on very specific locations, which is ideal if you know the town or city you want to be based in.

Jobs.ac.uk

Launched in 1998 by the University of Warwick, Jobs. ac.uk has become the leading international jobs board for careers in academic, research, science and related professions. It helps 700+ organisations worldwide to recruit highly qualified academic staff. If you are looking to stay on at university but in a paid role, this is a great tool to use in your search.

How to job search effectively

Knowing where to start can feel daunting and the recruitment process can be very long-winded, so start your search sooner rather than later to stay motivated.

Schedule time to research

Identify when you're at your most productive and allocate this time to job searching and submitting your applications. Research suggests that the first two hours after waking up are when people are most proactive, so set your alarm and get searching while you're feeling motivated. If you're more of a night owl, take some time each evening to focus on your search. Technology means that we have access to the internet on our phones any time, any place, so instead of checking up on social media or updating your Facebook status, use your downtime effectively and make use of the many job-search apps.

Invest in the roles that match your skill set

Save yourself time by applying for the right positions – ones that are a match for your skills, experiences and values. This will increase your chances of making it through the first part of the application process. It's vital to ask yourself if you're genuinely interested in the position you're applying for. Recruiters can always spot those applications that applicants have spent little time on, and they can tell when an applicant hasn't bothered to make sure their skills and experience match what's required in the role. Also, prioritise quality over quantity – submitting fewer well-presented, well-considered applications instead of multiple slapdash ones will help you secure the job of your dreams far quicker.

Keep track of what you're applying for

Use your phone or a notebook to keep a record of the applications and/or CVs you've submitted. This way, you'll know exactly what you've applied for and whom you have or haven't heard back from.

Some useful things to keep track of:

- The organisation who has the position (be mindful that this position could be available via a recruitment agency)

- The contact's name and telephone number (should you need to follow up)
- The position you're applying for
- The reference number
- The salary details
- The closing date

Visit www.sophiemilliken.co.uk/from-learner-to-earner-resources to download a job-search planner to help you stay organised.

Remain positive

We all get a few knock-backs while looking for work. Try not to take it personally if you're rejected or don't get a response from a recruiter. Your application simply might not match the criteria they're looking for – it's not a reflection of you as a person. Use these knock-backs as an opportunity to ask for feedback to develop your future applications.

How to use recruitment agencies as part of your search

Recruitment agencies exist to help employers source the best possible candidates for their available positions. Using a recruitment agency in your search can be really beneficial if you approach it in the right way.

What do recruitment agencies do?

A recruitment agency matches candidates to job vacancies. It works directly with organisations to help fill their roles. Consultants source opportunities directly with employers, generate CVs, and prepare candidates for interviews. In essence, they streamline the whole job-seeking process.

Find the right agency

Ask yourself these questions to help you narrow down your search and target the right agency:

- What types of employers work with the agency? Are they ones that you'd like to work for?

- Does the agency recruit for the types of positions you're searching for?

- Does the agency want to meet you in person? Over the phone? Or do they just want you to send your CV over? Meeting face-to-face will allow you to make the best impression, so do this where possible.

- What is the agency's reputation?

- What are other candidates saying about their experiences?

- What background checks will the agency need to perform on you?

Getting your relationship right

Figuring out which agency will fit your needs is often the best place to start. But once you've identified this, it's important to think about how you're going to work together.

- Make contact via phone and arrange to meet in person so you can build rapport and engage in a more personable way.

- Take along an up-to-date CV – make sure it shows off your skills and capabilities – and show interest in the work the agency does.

- Ask how your CV compares to those of other candidates.

- Agree on how often you'll communicate once you leave the office.

Recruitment agencies to consider

The following agencies are known in the graduate space:

Aspire

Formerly The Graduate Recruitment Company, Aspire specialises in the digital, media, events, and marketing and communications sectors. Established for over twenty-five years, they have access to a range of opportunities in their sector.

Celsius Graduate Recruitment

Provides specialist graduate recruitment services and ISMM-endorsed graduate sales training services to help graduates find graduate careers.

Freshminds

Sources graduates, researchers, analysts, consultants, project managers and directors for demanding permanent jobs or consulting projects. I have experience of working with them from my time at John Lewis and found that they worked well with both graduates and employers.

Graduate Fasttrack

A boutique consultancy working with an elite selection of employers in London and other parts of the UK. It specialises in placing graduates in sales and recruitment roles within media, IT, finance and property.

MyKindaFuture

MyKindaFuture only works with organisations that are committed to recruiting graduates and developing their careers. It covers all industry sectors, from sales and marketing, to HR and finance; engineering and technology to legal and consulting. It is active within the student employer community and highly regarded by employers.

Pareto

Offers a unique alternative to traditional recruitment agencies, taking you on the full journey from application through to assessment, training, placement and beyond.

Vine Graduate

Helps graduates secure entry-level roles within the recruitment sector in London, Manchester, Birmingham, Bristol and Leeds. It has a vast range of clients, from multinational recruiters to niche and boutique start-ups across all sectors.

Wiser Graduates

Introduces young people to companies that invest in their future, whether you're looking to innovate at a young start-up or enter the corporate world. The team offers advice and can introduce you to a wealth of roles to suit any degree type or skill set.

The dos, don'ts and how-tos of connecting with employers on LinkedIn

LinkedIn is a great tool for finding out all you need to know about organisations and the employees who work there. It's also a fantastic tool for making connections and growing your network so it includes employers that could offer you jobs in the future. But it's important to know the etiquette when connecting directly with employers. A good first impression could mean the difference between being ignored and landing the job you've always wanted.

EXPERT INSIGHT
'I'm more than happy for candidates to reach out. They need to call me by my name, though, and not the name used in their previous message to another recruiter.' (Ashley)

Here are some tips for approaching employers over LinkedIn.

Think quality over quantity – choose wisely

It's not necessary to connect with everyone who appears on your LinkedIn feed. Try to make connections with people who are working in the industry or sector you want to develop your career in. They may have similar skills, or experience in a field you're interested in. Or they may be the hiring manager or recruiter for a particular organisation. Just be sure you have some link to them.

Be polite and professional

The last thing you want is for a potential employer to think you're sloppy. Introduce yourself properly and remember you're talking to a potential employer, not your best friend. Ensure the tone of your message fits and shows you off in a good light.

Don't be afraid to connect

One of the main purposes of LinkedIn is to build business connections. So, if a hiring manager or recruiter is advertising a role that you're interested in, send them an invite to connect. Who knows, you could secure yourself an interview. At the very least, you'll build your professional network.

Hi <<their name>>

I have seen your posts on <<name of LinkedIn group>> and really like your points/perspective.

I Look forward to connecting in person.

Kind regards,

<<Your Name>>

Hi <<their name>>

I'm looking to expand my professional connections and would love to have you as part of my growing network.

Kind regards,

<<Your Name>>

Don't pester

If an employer accepts your invitation to connect, you might wish to send them a message to thank them for connecting (see above for examples of invitations to connect). But if you don't hear back from them, it's best not to pester – you're unlikely to secure a job irritating a potential employer.

Single focus or scattergun approach

Which is better: casting your net wide or narrowing your focus? I recommend that you start by thinking bigger picture. Gather your information, keep an open mind and be curious about what's available to you. Then, once you're armed with all your information and research, you can start to narrow down your search.

STUDENT CASE STUDY: LOUISE, UNIVERSITY OF BIRMINGHAM

I met Louise at a final stage assessment centre and interview. I asked her which other companies she had applied to. She told me no other company, as she was so committed to securing this role at John Lewis that she was putting everything into her application. She also told me that she knew she would be one of the strongest candidates I saw at this stage. I believed her – on both points. She was an outstanding candidate and had one of the highest sets of scores of all the offers I made that year. She was also the first in her cohort to be promoted, so her prediction was accurate. I've met other candidates who have admitted to me that they just picked up *The Times Top 100* book and applied to everyone they'd heard of on the list.

EXPERT INSIGHT

'I think a smaller number of high-quality applications beats "spray and pray" every time. As an ex-recruiter, I could always tell when a CV or application was a generic approach that had been sent to several companies with minimal alterations, and those candidates went straight onto the rejection pile. On the other hand, a well-researched application that showed why the candidate specifically wanted to work for my company would stand out from the crowd and catch my attention straight away. Those were the ones we invited to assessment centres.' (Gary)

I suggest applying for jobs with companies you have genuine enthusiasm for – and this number is unlikely to be huge. It can take hours to complete each application form, and that's before the days invested in attending assessment centres. So spend your time wisely. Put in strong and well-thought-out application forms that are more likely to get you to the next stage. A word of warning: if you do apply for anything and everything, not only will your conversion rate likely be lower, but you'll find it hard to show the passion and enthusiasm for each job at interview stage – a key factor in securing the job.

EXPERT INSIGHT

'Avoid a scattergun approach and make sure you tailor your application. I think if a candidate is applying for lots of roles but they are the same/similar then this is OK, but don't apply for anything and everything – best to focus your time on making fewer quality applications.' (Tonia)

Part One Summary

I hope that you now have a deeper understanding about what you're looking for from your career search, and that you've been able to explore what's important to you and build further knowledge about what you want from your future employer. With a greater awareness of your strengths and values, you have a picture of the type of job and employer you want, or at least the industry you'd like to work in.

Take time to reflect on what you've learned about yourself and the information you've reviewed. It's a long development journey, but it doesn't have to be boring and difficult. Instead, if you identify the right tools and people to help, it can be illuminating. It can enhance your self-awareness – an important behaviour that employers look for.

Here are some useful links to information on the top graduate employers. These might help you get a feel for an organisation's culture and values and help you identify if an organisation is right for you.

- Rate My Placement: The Top 100 Undergraduate Employers www.ratemyplacement.co.uk/top-employers

- Target Jobs: The UK 300 https://targetjobs.co.uk/uk300

- The Job Crowd: Top 100 Graduate Employers www.thejobcrowd.com/companies/top-100-graduate-employers

- The Times Top 100 Graduate Employers www.top100graduateemployers.com

MY TOP TIP

Apply early – over two-fifths of the UK's leading employers said they received more completed graduate job applications during the early part of the recruitment season than they did last year, and a third also believed the quality of applications had improved (High Fliers 2019).[22]

---

22 High Fliers Research Limited (2019) *The Graduate Market in 2019.*

PART TWO
GETTING A JOB OFFER

'One important key to success is self-confidence.
An important key to self-confidence is preparation.'
 — Arthur Ashe

Four
Early Stages Of The Assessment Process

The initial stages of the recruitment process are the hardest to pass. At this point there are often thousands of candidates, and only a manageable number can move through each stage. The rise in application numbers has led to employers using technology more frequently to help sift the candidates automatically through the different stages. It's often the case that you won't actually meet the employer until the final stage of the assessment process, so it can be a challenge to stand out.

Are you eligible?

First things first. Before you invest hours or days in a recruitment process for an employer, figure out if you're eligible to apply. Employers use something called 'killer questions' at the start of the process to cover some or all of the following: minimum degree requirement, UCAS points, work experience, right to work in the UK and location flexibility. If you don't meet these minimum criteria, the applicant tracking system will automatically reject you. There can be exceptions, but you'll need to contact the employer directly before beginning your online application. For example, there might be extenuating circumstances as to why you have lower UCAS points or a lower degree grade.

What to expect from the assessment process

The overwhelming majority of ISE employers characterise their recruitment approach as 'competency-based' (79%), but there are also substantial numbers that favour 'strengths-based' (43%), 'values-based' (32%) and 'technical' (40%) approaches to recruitment.[23] Most combine more than one approach, so candidates need to be ready to answer a range of questions and manage different selection activities.

---

23 Hooley, T (2018) *ISE Annual Student Recruitment Survey 2018.* https://ise.org.uk/page/ISEPublications, p9.

Selection and recruitment activities, ISE Annual Recruitment Survey 2018[24]

Selection and recruitment activities	% hiring graduates	% hiring apprentices
Assessment centres	89%	88%
Bespoke online applications	77%	60%
Psychometric tests	71%	51%
Face-to-face interviews	71%	71%
CV screening	66%	73%
Video interviews	49%	33%
Phone interviews	39%	14%

Looking at the table, we can make some basic assumptions. It's likely that the assessment process will start with your submitting an application form and/or a CV. Then you'll need to complete a test (or two or three!) and be interviewed via phone or video before attending an assessment centre and/or a final face-to-face interview.

Remember, before getting stuck into applying for jobs, make sure you've done your research. Identify which organisations you plan to apply to and educate yourself on the deadlines. It's also a good idea to do a social media audit to ensure all your profiles are professional (or set to private if they aren't employer friendly) and up to date.

---

24 Hooley (2018) *ISE Annual Student Recruitment Survey 2018*, p32.

Using LinkedIn to connect with the right people

Social media connects millions of people all over the world, and one of the most popular sites for professionals is LinkedIn. LinkedIn creates opportunities to build networks, promote your professional experience and develop links to professional communities. It can even help you find a job.

It can be hard to stand out in the current job market, but a LinkedIn profile will raise your personal profile and help you build your network. With a good profile, you can:

- **Create a professional brand that people can see:** It's the perfect opportunity to share your skills, qualities and knowledge with a huge audience that includes professionals, recruiters and future employers.

- **Increase awareness:** Through LinkedIn, you can keep up to date with relevant information and news about your areas of interest.

- **Generate ideas and take part in discussions:** This can grow your knowledge and enable you to explore new and exciting opportunities. Joining discussion groups allows you to meet likeminded people and share experiences.

- **Gain recommendations and endorsements:** LinkedIn offers a feature where you can ask people to recommend you. Ask for endorsements from lecturers or fellow students. People with recommendations have a greater chance of being noticed by potential employers.

- **Research your favourite organisations:** This is a great way to understand more about the organisations you'd like to work for, talk to the people who work in them or learn more about the industry and wider network.

- **Set up job alerts and receive notifications:** You can activate email alerts to receive notifications about jobs that match your skill set.

- **Help recruiters and employers find you:** Lots of recruiters use LinkedIn to search for new talent. If your profile is professional and detailed, it's more likely to attract attention – you might even get headhunted!

Your step-by-step guide to making the most of your profile

I've created a step-by-step guide to help you make the most of your profile, whether you're new to LinkedIn or wanting to freshen up an existing profile. Visit www. sophiemilliken.co.uk/from-learner-to-earner-resources to download a your copy of the guide and get networking in no time.

What makes an all-star profile

Setting up your profile isn't difficult, but if you want to stand out and represent yourself well, it's important to:

- Use a professional photo

- Create a headline that stands out from the crowd

- Complete the summary field using five or six of your key achievements

- Add images or documents to your experiences

- Ensure your profile is fully complete and has enough detail

- Keep your work history relevant

- Ask for recommendations

- Use status updates to share industry-relevant content

Take a tour of an effective LinkedIn profile – see how and why it works

If you need some inspiration, take a look at the profiles of prominent people in the companies that interest you. Here's a link to my LinkedIn profile: www.linkedin.com/in/sophie-milliken. Feel free to practise your invitation to connect by sending me a request.

Things to look out for while taking your tour:

- Notice the professional photo

- Read the profile headline: does it include the industry sector and location?

- What does the summary section say about the person?

- Is their current position, work experience and education complete and up to date?

- What skills and expertise have been identified?

- How many connections do they have?

- Explore their recommendations: what do they say about them?

Social media dos and don'ts

Social media is a great way to keep in touch with friends and share your exciting memories, but be aware that some recruiters will look up potential candidates on social media before making them a job offer. It's important to represent yourself well on all social media platforms. I've outlined the key dos and don'ts to help you.

The dos

- **Search for yourself on the internet:** You'll be amazed by how much information is captured on the internet. Make sure there's nothing on the first or second page of the search pages that could show you in a bad light. If there is, get it removed. Also check for images that might appear from old sites you no longer use.

- **Cleanse your social media profiles:** Getting rid of any social media content that doesn't show you in the best light is the easiest way to make sure recruiters and employers don't see it. I'm not saying you need to delete all your precious memories – just remove those that are less forgiving, or change your privacy settings.

- **Check your privacy settings:** If your Facebook, Twitter and Instagram accounts aren't suitable for public viewing, make sure they're private.

- **Be careful what you post:** You never know who might view your profiles, so don't post anything inappropriate. Keep it professional.

The don'ts

- **Hide:** Employers and recruiters will want to see that you have a social media presence, so don't go completely off-grid.

- **Post anything you wouldn't want your grandparents to see:** Keep it clean. Remember, information remains on the internet for a very long time.

- **Connect to everybody:** Think twice before accepting requests from friends on your LinkedIn account. Connections should be relevant to your industry.

- **Overshare:** Don't post anything that you'll regret later or that could damage your chances of securing the job of your dreams. Be mindful of what you share and how you share it.

EXPERT INSIGHT

'It's fine to connect with me on professional sites – LinkedIn being the obvious one. Not fine on personal sites – Facebook being the obvious one. The best examples are those candidates who not only connect on LinkedIn but interact with you – liking, commenting, sharing, etc – ie they build a relationship.' (David)

MY TOP TIP

Occasionally, computer systems do weird and not-so-wonderful things, so it's always best to save a copy of your finalised LinkedIn-profile content. It's so simple. Using a desktop computer, click on your LinkedIn-profile page, then click More (just below your name) and then Save to PDF.

Five
Creating Your Killer CV And Cover Letter

Writing a killer CV that grabs an employer's attention can be a difficult task, especially if you're starting from scratch, so this chapter includes many useful tips and suggestions to help.

Why is your CV important?

- Your CV is the first opportunity you have to make an impact and showcase who you are

- At least 50% of graduate CVs are rejected

- The average employer spends around 6.25 seconds reading a CV (even less if it doesn't grab their attention)

Does your CV include all the right things?

Your CV needs to include all the things that a future employer is looking for. It must show off your strengths, qualities and experience and give the reader a feel for the type of person you are. It's vital to get the basics right – ensure your layout is clear and well structured.

General

- Personalise the content (consider your experience, skills and strengths)

- Tailor the content each time you apply for a job, matching relevant skills and abilities

- Ensure your CV grabs the reader's attention

- Proofread for spelling, grammar and typos (consider getting someone else to do this for you)

- Make sure your CV is an honest reflection of you and your experiences – exaggerations and omissions can be found out at interview

- Avoid using acronyms and jargon

Layout and presentation

- You don't need a header saying 'CV' or 'Curriculum Vitae'

- Use bullet points to list information and highlight specific areas

- Make sure your CV isn't longer than two pages

- Print on white paper and in portrait mode, not landscape

- There are so many different fonts, but I recommend using Arial, Calibri, Times New Roman or Verdana

- A 12-point font is ideal, but you can go slightly smaller if you need the space (just make sure it's readable)

- Headings should separate each section of your CV (try using bold or CAPITALS for visual appeal)

- Your content and headings should be left aligned, not centred

- Use the Tab key rather than the space bar to indent information (this way, your indents match throughout)

- Always save your CV in MS Word format but send it as a PDF to the employer

Personal details

It's amazing how many people forget to include their name and address on their CV. Include this important personal information along with your contact number and email address. As mentioned, it's worth checking that your voicemail message and email address are appropriate and professional.

- You don't need to include your date of birth, nationality, marital status, national insurance number or passport number

- You don't need to include a headshot unless you've been asked to do so or it's an industry norm to do so (such as in some creative industries or for international jobs)

Personal profile

This appears at the top of your CV, so it needs to make you stand out from the crowd. It's your opportunity to sell yourself and what you can bring to your potential employer. In three or four lines, capture:

- Who you are

- What skills and qualities you can bring to the organisation

- What you're looking for in your career

- Why you're the most suitable candidate for the role

You may find the list of action words opposite useful when writing your profile. This list is also available to download at www.sophiemilliken.co.uk/from-learner-to-earner-resources.

Accomplished	Efficient	Persuasive
Accurate	Empathetic	Positive
Active	Encouraging	Practical
Adaptable	Energetic	Precise
Adventurous	Enterprising	Productive
Ambitious	Enthusiastic	Prudent
Analytical	Ethical	Qualified
Articulate	Flexible	Quick
Assertive	Focused	Rational
Attentive	Forceful	Realistic
Calm	Formal	Reflective
Capable	Goal Orientated	Reliable
Compassionate	Imaginative	Resourceful
Competent	Innovative	Responsible
Competitive	Insightful	Responsive
Concise	Intellectual	Self Assured
Confident	Intelligent	Self Confident
Conscientious	Logical	Self Controlled
Considerate	Mature	Self Reliant
Consistent	Methodical	Self Starting
Constructive	Meticulous	Sincere
Creative	Motivated	Strong
Decisive	Natural Ability	Sympathetic
Dependable	Observant	Systematic
Determined	Optimistic	Tactful
Diligent	Organised	Talented
Disciplined	Original	Tenacious
Eager	Patient	Thorough
Economical	Perceptive	Wise
Effective	Persistent	

Consider these two examples.

Bad example:

> I am a dynamic, passionate, enthusiastic student. I am also a great team leader and team player. I am looking for a graduate job after I graduate.

This profile is too brief and doesn't actually say anything (it's very vague). It includes some buzzwords but no evidence to support them.

Good example:

> I am a final-year student on track for a strong 2:1 in accounting at the University of Liverpool. My passion for a career in finance was ignited following my work experience at a local accountancy firm and nurtured through several relevant internships. The strong leadership skills developed through my extracurricular activities – treasurer of the Business Society and vice-captain of the rugby team – make me a strong candidate for a role in the KPMG graduate scheme.

This profile is strong. It's clear who the candidate is, and their passion appears more genuine with relevant evidence to support their aim. The candidate has tailored their profile to their application and included skills which would be attractive to an employer such as KPMG.

Employment history

This section should include all your relevant work experience (list your most recent first). Include job title, name of the organisation, dates employed and your key responsibilities.

- Use bullets when describing your duties (tailor the duties to match what the employer is looking for)

- List at least three key achievements – include quantitative data that supports them (any numbers or figures)

- Include any part-time and temporary work, highlighting the transferable skills that apply to the job

- You don't need to include salary details or reasons for leaving previous jobs

Education and qualifications

List your education and qualifications, including dates, type of qualification and grades you've achieved. You may not need to go as far back as secondary education if you have a lot of work experience.

- Avoid volunteering negative information (eg course started but not finished, failed exams, etc)

- List all relevant work-based training, such as NVQs, first aid or health and safety

- List any professional memberships you may hold (eg member of the Chartered Institute of Marketing)

Skills and achievements

Choose five or six skills the job is looking for and then provide your best example of each. Your skills and achievements should be relevant to the job you're applying for. Try ordering them in the level of importance according to the job role. Remember that skills can be gained from education, work, voluntary work and extracurricular activities.

To download a skills worksheet to use as a guide when writing your CV, visit www.sophiemilliken.co.uk/ from-learner-to-earner-resources.

Personal interests or hobbies

Mention only interests and hobbies that are relevant to the role you're applying for – ones that complement your skills and experience. Avoid including things such as 'socialising with friends' or 'going to the cinema', as these activities don't add any value to your CV.

Consider – could a hobby interfere with your work? Are there any conflicts of interest?

Remember: if it's not going to add value, it's better to leave it out.

Voluntary work

Including voluntary or unpaid work on your CV is a great way to show future employers that you're passionate and hard-working. It shows that you're willing to learn new skills and gain new experiences, and that you like to help and support other people.

References

It used to be necessary to include two references in your CV. These days, they're generally not required at this early stage of the application process.

You could include 'References available on request', but employers will ask for your references should you be successful – always check with referees before using their details.

MY TOP TIPS

To make your CV stand out from the crowd, make sure it's:

- Clearly formatted and presented
- Laid out in a logical order with headings (choose a professional font)
- Positive in tone
- Short and succinct – two pages is perfect
- Tailored to the role you're applying for
- Free of errors – check grammar and spelling thoroughly

Things to avoid including in your CV

- Height, weight and state of health
- Date of birth, marital status, nationality, family details
- Religious or political beliefs
- Jargon or abbreviations
- Attachments (additional qualifications, references, etc)
- Gimmicks
- Fancy borders that may not scan well
- Referee names and addresses
- Last or expected salary
- Reasons for leaving each job

Finally, don't fold or staple your CV, or print it double-sided.

EXPERT INSIGHT

'Less impressive are the "stock" answers, eg "socialising with friends". Anything on a CV should add value to your application, and a generic approach to extracurricular activities won't do this.' (David)

How to write a great cover letter

Your cover letter is an important tool. It's usually sent out to employers along with your CV. You can use your cover letter to emphasise how your skills and experience match what's required for the job. It's one of the easiest and most effective ways to stand out from the crowd, and brings to the table a little extra information about you and what you can offer the organisation.

Essential details

- Your personal details (eg name, address, email address, telephone number)
- The date you sent the letter
- The address of the organisation
- The hiring manager's name, if you have it – if you don't, write, 'Dear Sir / Madam'

- The job title and reference number (eg Graduate Consultant, Reference 34534095)

Essential content

- Where you found the vacancy and the date the job was advertised

- Why you're applying

- Your recent experience (a summary)

- Your skills and aspirations

- Why you want to work for the organisation – show that you've done your research; explain what's made this organisation stand out

- A summary of your interest in the job – close this paragraph with 'I look forward to hearing from you'

- A closing line: 'Yours sincerely' or 'Yours faithfully' (if you addressed the letter to Dear Sir / Madam, close with 'Yours faithfully'; if you addressed it to a specific person, close with 'Yours sincerely')

Remember, your CV should always:

- Draw attention to how well you measure up to the job requirements

- Highlight your relevant skills, qualifications and experience

- Be positive, clear and enthusiastic

My tried-and-tested CV and cover letter templates

There are so many templates to choose from – finding the perfect one can take a lot of time and energy. Visit www.sophiemilliken.co.uk/from-learner-to-earner-resources to download some templates to get you started. You can choose the format and style that's right for you.

TASK: Create your CV and cover letter

Choose the template most suitable for you and put together your CV and cover letter. Make good use of your careers service and arrange to have a CV check with an advisor so you can get feedback.

The application form: getting the basics right

The length of the recruitment process can be daunting. Maybe you're feeling as if you've already jumped through several hoops only to be faced with having to complete an application form.

STUDENT CASE STUDY: FATIMA, KINGSTON UNIVERSITY

'When I began my graduate job search, I was completely overwhelmed with the number of tasks that needed to be completed for each application. Some employers wanted me to complete four tests along with an application form and CV. It would take me hours to get through these stages for each employer. It got easier when I had completed a few applications, but I still don't completely understand why employers make students jump through so many hoops.'

If you're feeling overwhelmed, this comprehensive checklist will help you make sure you complete your application form successfully.

- Read and follow instructions fully (review the whole application briefly before making a start)

- Answer every question fully – don't rely on your CV to fill in the gaps

- Make sure your contact details are correct

- Check your email address to make sure it's ready for professional use

- Ensure your employment dates are accurate

- Outline your employment roles and responsibilities clearly, stating your successes and achievements

- Check that your qualifications are correctly detailed

- Avoid leaving blank spaces – if questions don't apply to you, respond with 'Not applicable'

- Proofread your application thoroughly – check for spelling, grammar and typing errors
- Always add something of value or relevance if there's an 'additional information' section (it never looks good to leave this blank)

A simple yet effective technique to tackle tricky questions

Competency-based questions are asked during various stages of the recruitment process – even featuring in the application form. These are questions which ask you to provide examples of things you've done in the past and which are linked to skills and attributes (eg being able to work in a team).

There's a tried-and-tested technique that will help you answer these tricky questions.

It's known as the STARR technique. Employers use these questions because they allow them to compare all the people who are applying for the job in a methodical and structured way. By using this step-by-step method, you'll be able to respond to each question in a systematic manner, without forgetting the important stuff.

SITUATION
Describe the situation you were in or the task you needed to accomplish

TASK
Describe the challenges and expectations. What needed to be done and why?

ACTION
Elaborate on your specific action. What exactly did you do and how did you do it?

RESULT
Explain the result, including your accomplishments, recognition and the outcome

REFLECTION
What did you learn about your approach, or about yourself? What would you do differently next time?

Which questions need a STARR response?

These questions will usually start along the lines of 'tell me about a time when you…' This will be followed by those competencies listed on the job specification or role profile, so it's important to be familiar with them so that you can prepare. Many graduate employers will want to know about soft skills such as teamwork, negotiation and communication.

A lot of the questions will require you to think about past work experience. If you're applying for internships or apprenticeships or have no previous work experience, you could refer to extracurricular activities, what you achieved while being a member of a university society, or school projects you've been involved in.

Let's look at the STARR response in detail:

Situation

This is about setting the scene – providing context and background. For example, if you're presented with a question about project management, your response would need to include:

- The details of the project you were working on

- With whom you were working

- When it happened and where you were

Task

This is about your specific role in the situation. You need to make sure that the assessor knows exactly what you were tasked with.

Action

This is the most important part of the STARR technique. You need to get across what you specifically did, so use 'I' rather than 'we' – otherwise it won't be clear exactly what *your* contribution was. Share a lot of detail as they won't be familiar with your history (but avoid acronyms and institutional language).

If you're asked to give an example of a time you dealt with a difficult client or customer, for example, you could explain how you decided to take a certain course of action to avoid making the situation worse or upsetting the individual.

Result

The result should be a positive one, and ideally one that can be quantified – for example, you secured repeat business, were responsible for an increase in sales by 12% or made a process four times more efficient.

Reflection

The employer will also want to know what you learned from that situation and if there's anything you'd do differently if faced with that situation again.

The STARR technique enables you to showcase your relevant experience in a methodical way. I recommend doing some in-depth preparation before starting the application process so that you have some great examples to use.

You will find a link to my 'Interview preparation using STARR' worksheet at www.sophiemilliken.co.uk/from-learner-to-earner-resources.

MY TOP TIPS

- A strong STARR technique will be clear and concise
- When describing your background, be brief but give enough contextual information for your story to make sense
- The result aspect of the STARR technique is critical – everything in your example leads to this outcome

There are some key questions you should prepare for, such as 'Tell me about yourself' and 'Why do you want the job?'. But a lot of candidates waste time trying to prepare for every question that could possibly be asked – this is torture, and it never works.

A better use of time would be to identify six key achievements and explore all the different elements they involved and how these elements could be used to answer different questions. For example, if you led a university society, you could refer to this to show how you worked as part of a team or how you influenced others – just adapt the achievement to the question.

Six
Online Tests

Psychometric tests aim to measure attributes such as intelligence, aptitude and personality. They provide potential employers with insight into how well you work with other people, how well you handle stress and whether you'll be able to cope with the intellectual demands of the job.

Tests fall into two main categories: personality tests, which measure aspects of your personality, and aptitude tests, which measure your intellectual and reasoning abilities.

Personality tests

The idea behind these tests is that it's possible to quantify your personality by knowing how you felt, thought and behaved in a variety of situations (both at work and outside of work).

You'll be presented with statements about ways of feeling or acting and asked to respond to them. For example:

1. I prefer to avoid conflict

    a) true   b) false

2. I enjoy parties and other social occasions

    a) strongly disagree   b) disagree   c) neutral
    d) agree e) strongly agree

The number of questions you'll be expected to answer can vary from 50 to 200. You can't really prepare for these tests other than to be aware of the different types. Stay true to your personality and values and don't try to predict what the employer is looking for. If you second-guess the employer, you might not get the 'right' answers anyway, and if you end up getting the job, you might find it isn't a good fit for you.

Aptitude tests

There are at least 5,000 aptitude and ability tests on the market. Some of them contain only one type of question (for example, questions involving verbal or numerical reasoning) while others are made up of different types. Aptitude tests consist of multiple-choice questions and are administered under exam conditions. They are strictly timed, and a typical test might allow thirty minutes for approximately thirty questions.

The various types of tests include the following.

Verbal reasoning

These include questions about spelling, grammar and your ability to understand analogies and follow detailed written instructions. These questions appear in most general aptitude tests because employers usually want to know how well you can communicate.

Numerical ability

These include questions about basic arithmetic, number sequences and simple mathematics. In management-level tests, you'll often be presented with charts and graphs to interpret. These questions appear in most general aptitude tests because employers usually want some indication of your ability to use numbers, even if doing so isn't a major part of the job.

Abstract reasoning

These include questions that measure your ability to identify the underlying logic of a pattern and then determine the solution. Because abstract-reasoning ability is believed to be the best indicator of fluid intelligence and your ability to learn new things quickly, these questions appear in most general aptitude tests.

Spatial ability

These include questions that measure your ability to manipulate shapes in two dimensions or to visualise three-dimensional objects presented as two-dimensional pictures. These questions aren't usually found in general aptitude tests unless the job specifically requires good spatial skills.

Mechanical reasoning

These tests are designed to assess your knowledge of physical and mechanical principles. Mechanical-reasoning questions are used to select candidates for jobs such as those in the military (Armed Services Vocational Aptitude Battery), police forces and fire services, as well as candidates for many craft, technical and engineering occupations.

Fault diagnosis

These tests are used to select technical personnel who need to be able to find and repair faults in electronic and mechanical systems. As modern equipment of all types becomes more dependent on electronic control systems (and arguably more complex), the ability to approach problems logically to find the cause of the fault is increasingly important.

Data checking

These tests measure how quickly and accurately errors can be detected in data and are used to select candidates for clerical and data-input jobs.

Work sample

Sometimes candidates may be asked to do a sample of the work that's required in the job. This may involve exercises using a word processor or spreadsheet, if the job is administrative, or it may involve giving a presentation or an in-tray exercise if the job is management or supervisory level.

Completing the tests

Don't be tempted to cheat! Be aware that you might need to redo your online tests in person.

Make sure you complete the tests on your own and don't ask for help from friends or family. Remember: the tests are about your ability, not that of another person. Some employers ask successful candidates to resit the tests when they attend an assessment centre or interview. This way, they can ensure that the scores add up and the test results are accurate and true.

Click the links below to make use of several practice tests.

- GraduateWings: www.graduatewings.co.uk/try-free-tests

- Practice Aptitude Tests: www.practiceaptitudetests.com

- Job Test Prep: www.jobtestprep.co.uk/graduate-management-aptitude-tests

- Psychometric Success: www.psychometric-success.com/downloads/download-practice-tests.htm

- SHL: www.shldirect.com/en/practice-tests

I've seen many candidates complain when they fail at the test stage, but this example from a recruiter contact of mine is priceless: 'One of the candidates failed his verbal and numerical reasoning. He said that he was burgled, and it was the burglar who took the test!'

Practice makes perfect. You only get one chance at the tests, so make sure you know what to expect and you'll have the advantage over others.

Seven
Tackling Telephone And Video Interviews

As society continues to embrace the digital world, more and more employers are using telephone or video interviews as part of their application process. At this stage, employers want to ensure that the strongest candidates make it through to the assessment centre or final interview.

Why are recruiters using these interviewing methods?

- They allow recruiters to see more people in less time (which is important given the high numbers of applicants applying for roles).

- They allow recruiters to test you on your CV and application form to see if the information you've included adds up.

- They allow recruiters to measure communication skills – they'll pay attention to how well you conduct yourself and respond to their questions.

- Video interviews enable recruiters to see an applicant's flare or personality (this is especially important in the creative industries).

- They support those recruiters who need to conduct interviews long distance.

What to expect in a telephone interview

Often, graduate recruiters will want to carry out a first interview over the telephone. Knowing what to expect from this call and being prepared should always be at the top of your agenda.

- Telephone interviews typically last around twenty to thirty minutes, so you need to be succinct with your responses.

- Usually there's only one interviewer.

- Your interview may be recorded, but the interviewer should make you aware of it if this is the case.

- You'll likely be asked questions based on your CV, work experience and education.

- Typically, competency-based interview questions will be asked in order to draw out your skills, experience and knowledge. These could include:

  - Why are you applying for this position?

  - What do you know about the organisation?

  - What are your greatest achievements?

  - What are your career ambitions?

Check out the 'Interview preparation using STARR worksheet' available at www.sophiemilliken.co.uk/ from-learner-to-earner-resources to help you structure your responses.

What to expect in a video interview

Pre-recorded video interviews are rapidly becoming popular among graduate recruiters. According to a recent survey carried out by the ISE, 49% of organisations are now using them as part of the selection process.[25]

Pre-recorded video interviews are commonly used where there is high-volume recruitment for graduate roles. There is a small chance that you might have to complete a live video interview, particularly if the role is in another country and you are at the final stage

---

25 Hooley, T (2018) *ISE Annual Student Recruitment Survey 2018.* https://ise.org.uk/page/ISEPublications, p32.

of the process. In this situation, think about how you are dressed, bearing in mind the guidance in Chapter Nine. Here's what you can expect from a video interview:

- You'll likely be sent an invite to log in to a system, where you can access the video link and instructions

- You'll be asked to answer a series of pre-recorded questions

- Video interviews typically last around thirty minutes

- It will be recorded

- There's often the opportunity to have a practice run, so you can get used to the system and format

- You'll likely be asked questions based on your CV, work experience and education

- Typically, competency-based interview questions will be asked in order to draw out your skills, experience and knowledge

- Some employers will present candidates with different workplace situations and ask them to respond using one or all of these methods:

    - Answering multiple-choice questions

    - Recording yourself speaking

    - Typing your response

MY TOP TIPS

For a great video interview experience:

- Be prepared – get practising

- Remain professional

- Dress to impress

- Engage with your camera not the screen

- Have a backup plan should your internet connection fail

If you want to practise or learn more, check out these links:

www.sonru.com

www.launchpadrecruits.com/video-assessment

www.shineinterview.com

Common mistakes to avoid during a telephone or video interview

There are a few common mistakes that often mean the difference between ruining your chances and moving to the next stage. Some important things to avoid:

- Using slang words or abbreviations (the interviewer may not understand what you're talking about)

- Taking your call in an unsuitable location (eg in public or on the bus)

- Forgetting your scheduled interview

- Swearing

- Being interrupted or getting distracted

- Eating or chewing gum

- Running out of phone or laptop battery midway through the interview

Also make sure you don't smoke, talk about yourself in the third person or accidently say 'love you, bye' when finishing the call!

EXPERT INSIGHTS

Video interview company Shine shared an example from one of their clients, who told them of a candidate who ended up swearing at their mum on video. The candidate apparently answered the question they were asked, then their mum (who was sitting in the room while the candidate recorded their interview) helpfully chimed in with, 'Well I wouldn't have said that,' before the candidate had stopped the recording. The candidate's reaction, while still recording, was to call their mum a few things that you'd certainly not expect someone to call their mother!

An employer contact of mine, Paul, watched a video interview where the candidate's webcam fell to a ninety-degree angle. Instead of taking a few seconds to adjust the camera, the candidate just tilted his head to the side and continued that way for the rest of the recording.

Phillipa, an HR director based in the Middle East, interviewed someone who was having technical issues with their video so called in their housemate – who came in naked. 'There were two other assessors on the call with me. At least it broke the ice between us. In case you're wondering – the naked guy (when he realised he was on camera) tried to protect his dignity with the curtain!'

Opportunities to impress and stand out

There are many things you can do to prepare for a telephone interview. Here are a few things that might help you make an impression.

- Do your research: look at both the job role and the organisation you're applying to – what stands out?

- Have a copy of your CV and application form to hand so you know what you've submitted already.

- Have a notepad and pen ready, so you can make notes as you go.

- Prepare your answers: think about the typical questions you may be asked and how you might respond to these.

- Write down any questions you'd like to ask: at the end of your interview, you're likely to be asked if you have any questions, so ask something that will make you stand out.

- Get rid of any distractions: turn off the TV or radio and ensure you're in a private space. There's nothing worse than your flatmate or parents walking in while you're in the middle of a conversation.

A few additional things to consider when preparing for a video interview:

- Organise your surroundings: the recruiter will be able to see things around you, so make sure your surroundings are tidy and presentable.

- Dress appropriately: if you're applying for a creative role, you may want to dress more fashionably and creatively, otherwise smart and professional is perfect.

- Test your equipment: make sure your camera and computer are working correctly and your internet speed and sound quality are good before your call. There's nothing worse than a call that keeps losing connection.

How to answer the most challenging questions

Here are some ways to respond to common questions, to get you started.

What do you know about the company?

What to say: Provide a brief overview of the organisation – identify mission, values or cultural characteristics that stand out to you. Consider any figures or dates that are significant.

What not to say: 'Not that much as I haven't done any research.'

Talk me through your CV

What to say: Briefly summarise your education and work history – highlight key achievements and successes that you're proud of.

What not to say: Don't give lots of detail and go over every single point in your CV.

What interests you about the role you've applied for?

What to say: Demonstrate what you know about the position and the organisation, and try to match your skills and experiences to parts of the job description. Talk about why you think you're the best person for the role. This is a brilliant opportunity to get your passion, personality and values across, so take it.

What not to say: 'The salary is good' or 'I need a job'.

What experience do you have that makes you a suitable candidate?

What to say: Talk about your education/work experience that supports the job description and shows what duties and responsibilities you've carried out.

What not to say: 'I made the tea and emptied the bins.'

There seems to be a gap in your education/work experience – can you explain why?

What to say: Be honest, but be mindful of what details you share – keep it professional.

What not to say: Don't lie, as you'll get found out.

What are your career goals for the future?

What to say: Show passion for personal development – you want to showcase your commitment and strengths.

What not to say: 'Doing my job' – this can come across as cocky and arrogant.

Do you have any questions?

What to say: Make sure you've prepared some questions to ask (ask questions that show an interest in the organisation and role and in your own career development)

What not to say: 'No, I don't have any' or 'We've covered them already'.

When it comes to answering competency-based questions, in any type of interview, try to use the STARR technique. Lay out the situation you were facing, the task you had to do, the action you took and the result:

- **Situation:** Outline the situation

- **Task:** Talk about the task – what was required of you?

- **Action:** What did you do? What action/s did you take and why?

- **Result:** Summarise the results of your actions

- **Reflection:** What did you learn? What would you do differently in the future?

Doing this will help you show your relevant experience in a clear, concise and confident manner.

Simple etiquette to avoid awkwardness

In any interview situation, it's important to show the best you – telephone and video interviews are no exception. The interview is the first opportunity to speak directly with the recruiter, so you want to make sure it goes well.

Here's how:

- Be polite and professional at all times

- Ensure your space is quiet and free of distraction

- Address the interviewer by name (call someone else to find out what it is if you don't know it – addressing the caller as Mr Smith or Mrs Smith helps to build that relationship)

- No matter how excited you are about the job or how eager you are to share all your wonderful experiences, try not to interrupt – it will come across rude and as if you aren't listening

- Avoid using speakerphone, as this can cause interference and make it sound as though you're busy doing something else at the same time

- A recruiter's time is precious, so be mindful of time and succinct in your responses

- Be curious about the next steps – don't end the call without knowing when you might hear back from them or what the next step is should you be successful

- After your conversation, send a thank-you email or LinkedIn message to the recruiter (this will make you stand out from other applicants)

MY TOP TIPS

To show the best 'you':

- Take your time, stay calm and don't speak too fast

- Be polite, smile and avoid using any slang

- Be confident and professional

- Do your research and know why you're attracted to the organisation/role

- Have your CV, application form and job description to hand

- Be prepared

- Make notes

- Ask questions

Eight
Assessment Centres

Preparing for an interview alone can be a daunting prospect, but when an employer invites you to attend an assessment centre, knowing where to start and what to expect can be downright nerve-racking.

EXPERT INSIGHT

'Assessment centres are specifically designed to use a variety of tests and exercises to assess a range of different skills, and it's quite unusual for one candidate to perform brilliantly on every exercise. Inevitably some exercises will suit you more than others, and I remember plenty of examples in our "wash up" meetings where the business decided to hire a candidate who had underperformed on one exercise but recovered to show their potential on the others. We used a competency scoring grid for this very reason: if you didn't do a great job communicating during our written exercise, for example, we would also assess your communication skills during the interview and the group exercise – giving you multiple chances to impress.' (Gary)

What to expect

Many employers use assessment centres to gain as much information as possible about how a candidate is likely to perform on the job. Through a number of activities, they assess a candidate's skills, knowledge and behavioural fit for the organisation.

They're held either at an employer's offices, a local hotel or a training facility, so make sure you check the location and plan your journey accordingly. Assessment centres are hosted over a half day or a full day, depending on the role and industry, and you'll usually be joined by several other candidates (typically between six and twelve). It's important to balance being a team player with showcasing your own performance.

You'll be required to work both as an individual and as part of a group on a number of activities, which could include:

- Case studies

- Presentations

- Analytical exercises

- One-to-one or panel interviews

- Group exercises

- Role-play exercises

- Skills / written tests

- Psychometric tests

You'll likely complete three or four activities during the assessment centre. A typical assessment day might look like this:

09:00	Arrival, welcome and introductions
09:15	Employer presentation including format of the assessment
09:30	Ice breaker
09:45	Psychometric test
11:00	Individual task – In Tray Exercise
12:30	Lunch
13:15	Group exercise – Case Study
14:45	Individual presentations
15:30	Assessment interviews
17:00	Assessment debrief and next steps
17:30	Finish

You'll probably be introduced to assessors (recruiters and managers from within the organisation). These assessors will score your performance against a competency framework.

Assessors will be looking for you to show a variety of key skills and competencies throughout the assessment centre. Every activity will be focused on your ability to demonstrate these skills successfully. I've identified the most common skills employers look for:

Adaptability	Analytical Thinking	Commercial Awareness
Communication	Creativity	Critical Thinking
Decision Making	Flexibility	Leadership
Motivation	Negotiation	Organisation
Persuasion	Planning	Problem Solving
Resilience	Teamwork	Time Management

Often, assessors will discuss all aspects of a candidate's performance before making a decision. The outcome will generally be decided once all assessments have taken place, so don't expect to hear from them for at least a couple of weeks. Usually, the employer will inform you of when you should expect to hear back. When you know the outcome, be sure to ask for feedback, especially if you aren't successful. This will help you to identify what you need to work on in preparation for the next assessment centre.

EXPERT INSIGHT

'It's possible to bomb in one exercise but still pass the day. The whole aim of an assessment centre when it works effectively is to allow a range of assessors to see the candidate in a variety of exercises – the wash up then allows the scores to be reviewed and a discussion to take place that really teases out and considers how that candidate performed across the whole day. Typically, some exercises hold more "weight" than others too.' (Helen)

The types of exercises (and how to be ready for them)

Here are some of the key exercises you might face during an assessment centre.

Group exercises

Group exercises will usually involve between four and eight candidates, depending on the number of candidates attending the assessment centre. The employer will provide an industry- or workplace-related problem that requires a solution. Candidates are assessed against criteria designed to identify key competencies, including teamwork, leadership, enthusiasm, decisiveness, persuasiveness, problem-solving, critical thinking, communication and commercial awareness.

Some typical group exercises include:

- **Ice-breakers:** Aimed at relaxing candidates and building team spirit, these exercises are very popular. You might be asked to complete a task such as building a tower from straws and paper, and then using it to balance an egg or marshmallow.

- **Group discussions:** You'll be given a scenario and asked to reach a logical conclusion. Usually, candidates will be asked to lead the discussion in turn.

- **Case studies:** You'll be provided with a role to play based on background information and a brief. One common example is a mock meeting, where each candidate assumes a specific function and is expected to fulfil individual and group objectives.

I've worked with students who assumed that because they weren't extravert or naturally creative, they weren't good in a teamwork situation. In this case, I recommended exploring the popular research completed by Dr Meredith Belbin, who discovered that there are nine clusters of behaviour needed to create a high-performing team. Each role has its strengths and weaknesses, and each has equal importance.[26]

Once they understood which of the Belbin team roles they fell into, students had a greater understanding of their role, increased confidence and a better idea of how they could contribute. If you want to understand your role within a team better, take a look at the Belbin website – https://www.belbin.com/about/belbin-team-roles.

During group exercises, ensure that you:

---

26 Belbin (no date) 'The Nine Belbin Team Roles'. www.belbin.com/about/belbin-team-roles

- Get involved – make your points clearly and confidently

- Don't criticise, interrupt or undermine others, but do politely intervene if someone is dominating the group

- Follow instructions carefully, relating everything back to your brief

- Identify a timekeeper and a note-taker

- Involve other candidates, especially those who are quieter and more reserved

- Delegate appropriately, choosing the best person for each task

- Praise and show appreciation for others – build upon their comments

- Stand up for your opinion if criticised, putting forward relevant facts

- Remain calm but work quickly and decisively

STUDENT CASE STUDY: RACHNA, UNIVERSITY OF MANCHESTER

'I attended the assessment centre for a large retailer, and they had two group exercises as part of the day. These exercises were both really fun! In one exercise, we were given a load of people management issues and had to discuss these as a group and make recommendations as to what action we would take as the manager. It caused some lively debate, and one group member was really overbearing. I took the opportunity to try and bring quieter group members of the team into the discussion, which also had the benefit of calming the dominant guy a little. I received great feedback on taking this approach.'

Case studies

Case-study exercises are often used by consulting and accountancy organisations. They test your analytical skills, your problem-solving skills and your creativity.

The employer will describe a situation and you'll need to respond with advice in the form of a report or verbal explanation. You'll reach your conclusion by collating and analysing provided information.

Here are the sorts of questions you may be asked in a case study:

- Which of the three proposals should be implemented and why?

- Should the organisation invest in product A or product B and why?

- Is the merger between company A and company B a good idea and why?

- Is the way to drive profit through an online presence or by increasing high-street stores?

- Which target market has the largest revenue potential and why?

Make sure that you:

- Can justify your answers and defend your decisions
- Analyse the issue by looking for patterns, inconsistencies and contradictions
- Manage your time carefully
- Pay attention to detail
- Read all instructions and materials before you start, to understand what's expected of you
- Treat the task like a course assignment – arrange your material and draw conclusions

Presentations

Presentations assess your ability to communicate clearly with your audience. The skills that are being tested here are timing, engagement, creativity and ability to deliver a message. Presentations usually last between ten and twenty minutes, finishing with an opportunity for assessors to ask questions. Employers might ask you to prepare your presentation in advance, or you might be given the topic on the day and a short time to prepare.

How to prepare your presentation

- Focus on the key aims and objectives of the topic and tailor your presentation accordingly

- Ensure you have structure – include an introduction, a main section and a conclusion

- Show evidence of further research throughout your presentation

- Consider using reading cards to remember key messages and figures

- Keep information relevant and succinct – use bullet points and short sentences

- Stay on topic

- Use visual aids, flip charts, PowerPoint and handouts to keep your audience engaged

- Practise out loud beforehand and time yourself

- Be prepared for questions

When giving your presentation

- Smile and engage with your audience

- Maintain eye contact (don't just look at your notes)

- Keep calm and breathe

- Speak clearly and don't talk too fast

- Vary the tone of your voice

- Don't fidget

- Manage your time effectively

Here are a few examples of presentation topics you might come across:

Presenting on your background

'Tell us about an achievement that you're particularly proud of.'

'Why do you want to apply to us?'

'Why should we hire you?'

Presenting on company-focused topics

'How would you improve our business strategy over the next five years?' 'What do you think are the main challenges you may face in this role?'

'Carry out a SWOT analysis on our organisation.'

'What do you perceive our development areas to be and what recommendations would you make to address these?'

'Bring a new product to market: what's your strategy?'

In-tray or e-tray exercises

In-tray exercises are also known as inbox exercises or e-tray exercises (if completed digitally). This type of exercise requires you to organise a workload. It assesses key competencies such as analytical skills, decision-making, time management, accuracy, organisation and communication skills.

These exercises will usually take around thirty to sixty minutes to work through and will require you to explore ten to thirty items of paperwork, such as emails, faxes, letters, memos, minutes, reports, organisation charts, policy documents and telephone messages.

Your task will be to prioritise the items and explain what action is required for each. You may be asked to respond to queries, draft replies, make decisions or delegate tasks. You may also be given new material throughout the exercise.

To be successful, ensure that you:

- Know how you'll be assessed, and whether you can write on the documents

- Note the objectives in bullet form, paying attention to detail and referring to the material provided

- Prepare to justify your decisions

- Read all instructions and accompanying materials carefully before starting, and then make a rough plan based on any identifiable key issues

- Work quickly, accurately, systematically and logically

Role-play exercises

Role-play exercises are often used to assess candidates who are applying for customer-facing positions or management roles. Typically, these exercises are conducted one-to-one between a candidate and an assessor. The types of skills assessed are communication, leadership, negotiation and persuasion. You can often identify which skills are being assessed by the topic you've been asked to role-play. For example, if the scenario is based on selling something, then the assessor will be looking at your ability to influence and negotiate.

Here are some tips to help you prepare for role-play:

- Stay relaxed and keep calm
- Be yourself and behave how you would if the scenario were real
- Speak clearly and try not to rush
- Engage with the person role-playing with you; keep eye contact
- Research the role during your preparation time
- Keep to time

STUDENT CASE STUDY: JESSICA, LONDON SOUTH BANK UNIVERSITY

'I did a role-play in one of the assessment centres I attended last year. It was really scary! I had some information about a customer complaint and had to go into a room and deal with the situation. The person playing the customer was an actor, I think, and very convincing! I just tried to get into character using the information I'd been given and played my role as best as I could. I wouldn't say I enjoyed this task, but when I got into it, it was OK and I did pass the assessment day, so I must have done better than I thought.'

Skills/written tasks

This type of exercise usually involves writing an essay, an email, a letter or a report on a given topic, though you may sometimes be asked to proofread, review or summarise a document. These exercises typically take between forty and sixty minutes. They assess your common sense, reading comprehension and written communication.

Ensure that you:

- Read all the instructions and materials carefully

- Use a combination of headings, bullet points and writing styles to add emphasis

- Use acronyms only after you've explained them

- Use correct spelling and grammar

- Write for someone who doesn't have your knowledge

As you can see, there are a variety of exercises that the employer could choose to use. Remember that, regardless of the type of exercise, they are all aimed at giving you an opportunity to showcase the competencies, skills or values needed for the job. For example, if the employer has said that commercial awareness is needed for the role, think about how you can demonstrate this in the exercise.

MY TOP TIPS

To stand out from the crowd, it's important that you:

- Are assertive during all exercises

- Don't dwell on any mistakes; instead, concentrate on performing well in the next task

- Ensure that the assessors can see your working methodology

- Don't worry about the other candidates; focus on putting your key skills forward

- Draw others into group discussions

- Understand the requirements of each task – quickly digest the brief and then revisit it once you understand the overall challenge

- Join in with discussions, even at informal times (such as during meals) – ask other candidates about university if you're struggling for conversation

- Maintain a friendly and polite manner with everyone you meet and remember that you're always being assessed

- Relax and let your personality shine, as assessors warm to individuality

---

EXPERT INSIGHT

'We are assessing for five key competencies and we mark five exercises. These exercises cover one-to-one, group work, presentation, role-play – and there is always more than one exercise to demonstrate competence. So if role-plays aren't your thing, you may not score as well as in a group exercise, and thus your competence scores will balance throughout the AC. ACs shouldn't be about assessing your ability to be good at ACs – they should be about assessing your ability to be good in the role! Applicants should try not to 'self-assess', ie avoid the "I've screwed that up". If I had a pound for every time someone scored highly when they thought they'd "screwed up", I'd be retired to the Maldives by now!' (David)

Nine
The Face-To-Face Interview

Whether you're taking part in an interview as part of an assessment centre or have been invited to attend an interview separately, the same principles apply.

I'm going to share with you some best practices when it comes to preparing for and applying yourself at the interview. Face-to-face interviews are one of the most common parts of a selection process and are carried out with either one interviewer or a panel of several.

Preparation before the interview

Regardless of the type of interview you're preparing for, do your research and prepare thoroughly beforehand. This will give you the best possible chance on the day of your interview. Some important things to help you prepare:

- Identify the skills and experiences that the organisation is looking for by reviewing its website and social media platforms

- Understand the organisation's values, principles and culture

- Plan your journey in advance – it's always best to be early (where possible, complete a 'dry run' beforehand)

- Prepare answers to the most common questions employers ask

- Be prepared to ask your own questions at the end of the interview

- Find out about the people who will be interviewing you

- Research the issues, trends and opportunities affecting the organisation and the wider markets

- Consider how you'll overcome challenging questions, such as those about gaps in your work history or potential pitfalls in your CV or application

- On the night before your interview, avoid alcohol, prepare your outfit and get plenty of sleep

- On the morning of your interview, eat a healthy breakfast and don't consume too much caffeine (you can combat nerves by exercising, if you have time, as this creates feelings of well-being)

What to take with you:

- A bottle of water (and money, in case you need to buy water)

- A notebook and a pen

- Right-to-work ID – usually photo ID such as your passport or driving licence

- The job description and person specification

- Any academic certificates or training certificates

- Your CV, application form and interview invitation

The types of questions you may be asked

Many graduate employers use either competency-based or strengths-based questions as part of their recruitment process.

We're going to explore some questions you might be faced with and how to prepare for them.

Competency-based interviews

Competency-based interviews, which can also be known as structured, behavioural or situational interviews, are designed to test several skills or competencies. The interviewer will have a list of set questions and will compare your answers to predetermined criteria.

These interviews work on the basis that past behaviour is the best indicator of future performance. They're used by employers across all sectors but are particularly favoured by large graduate recruiters as part of their assessment-centre process.

A competency-based interview is systematic, and each question targets a skill needed for the job.

Some key competencies regularly used by employers include:

Adaptability	Decisiveness	Problem Solving
Communication	Independence	Organisation
Commercial Awareness	Flexibility	Teamwork
Conflict Resolution	Leadership	

You'll need to answer the questions in the context of previous experience or real-life events. The skills being tested will depend largely on the job you're interviewing for and the industry or sector you'll be working in.

You should expect questions to open with 'tell us about a time when you…', 'give an example of…' or 'describe how you…'.

You can find my competency-based example questions at www.sophiemilliken.co.uk/from-learner-to-earner-resources.

How to answer competency-based questions

You will be best placed to answer these types of questions using the STARR technique, which is covered in detail in Chapter Five. (See the diagram below.)

Using the STARR technique will ensure that you have some great examples ready for your interview.

EXPERT INSIGHT

'I remember interviewing a candidate who had mentioned on his application form that he had recently helped to plan his sister's wedding. When I asked him about it, he used the experience to create the most amazing example: he had a client (his sister!), a very firm deadline, various suppliers and an endless stream of changes to deal with: basically, he had done all the things a good project manager would do. Plus, the "project" had been a success! Not only was he able to demonstrate a great set of transferable skills, he also really made an impression on me – I can still picture that interview fifteen years later. And yes, he got the job, and became a very successful project manager.' (Gary)

SITUATION
Describe the situation you were in or the task you needed to accomplish

TASK
Describe the challenges and expectations. What needed to be done and why?

ACTION
Elaborate on your specific action What exactly did you do and how did you do it?

RESULT
Explain the result, including your accomplishments, recognition and the outcome

REFLECTION
What did you learn about your approach, or about yourself? What would you do differently next time?

Strengths-based interview

A strengths-based interview allows you to focus on what you *enjoy* doing, rather than on what you *can* do.

The theory is that by matching your strengths to the role, you'll be happier in your work, perform better, learn quicker and stay with the organisation for longer.

Unlike competency-based interviews, strengths-based interviews feel more informal and personal and allow employers to gain insight into candidates' personalities to see if they would be a good 'fit' for the company.

Top fifteen strengths-based interview questions to consider

Take some time to think about how you might respond to these questions:

1. Tell me about yourself

2. What energises you?

3. Do you prefer to focus on details or the bigger picture?

4. What is your greatest strength?

5. What is your greatest weakness?

6. What is your proudest achievement?

7. What do you enjoy doing the least?

8. How do you feel about deadlines?

9. How do you handle stress or pressure?

10. How do you evaluate success?

11. How do you stay motivated?

12. Why do you want this job?

13. Why are you the most suitable candidate?

14. What are your career goals?

15. How do you develop yourself?

How to answer strengths-based interview questions

It's important to know that strengths-based questions don't have right or wrong answers. But you must answer the questions honestly. Making information up will give the interviewer a false impression of you, and you could get found out later.

Include examples to back up and illustrate your responses. You can use examples from all areas of your life, including your studies, work experience, previous employment, voluntary or extracurricular activities.

Candidates often get caught out by questions that ask them to identify their weaknesses. Stay away from generic responses. For example, 'I'm a perfectionist' can come across as a little arrogant. Instead, think of things that you've struggled with – show some vulnerability and select real weaknesses. Make sure you explain how you used your strengths to overcome these weaknesses.

Interviewers will be taking note of your body language and tone of voice, which can provide insight into your sincerity. If you're genuinely describing something you enjoy, you'll be animated, and your enthusiasm and motivation will shine through.

Take a look at my strengths-based example questions at www.sophiemilliken.co.uk/from-learner-to-earner-resources.

What questions should you ask?

Asking questions at the end of your interview is just as important as answering questions during the interview. This is your opportunity to find out more about the role and organisation. Now is your chance to quiz the interviewer (obviously in the right way). Demonstrate why you're the most suitable candidate and stand out from your competitors. If you don't ask any questions, you run the risk of the interviewer thinking you're not interested in the role or not prepared. It's perfectly fine to write these questions on a notepad that you bring in to the interview. Make sure you don't ask questions that you can easily find the answers to yourself or that cover topics which have already been addressed in the assessment process.

Here are some great questions to ask your interviewer. You don't need to ask all of these. Select two or three that stand out to you:

- Can you tell me more about the day-to-day responsibilities of the role?

- What are your expectations of the successful candidate within the first three months of their being in the role?

- How could I impress you in my first three months?

- What are the biggest opportunities or problems the organisation is currently facing?

- What challenges could the successful candidate face in this role?

- What is the organisation's future strategy?

- How would you describe the organisation's working environment and culture?

- What do you enjoy most about working here?

- How is performance measured within the role or organisation?

- How do I compare with other candidates you've interviewed?

- Is there anything you were looking for that I haven't talked about?

- What is the typical career path for someone in this role?

- What personal development opportunities are available?

- What are the next steps in the interview process?

Questions to avoid:

- What is the salary for this position?

- What does your organisation do?

- When can I start taking time off?

- What holidays would I be entitled to?

- Do you go out drinking after work?

Ways to make an impact and stand out

Here are some simple ways to make an impact and stand out to your interviewers.

Be positive: Be polite and professional with any staff you meet before or after the interview. During the interview, avoid talking about any personal problems unless completely necessary, and never talk badly about your previous employers.

Pay attention to your body language: Give the interviewer a firm handshake both when you arrive and before you leave your interview. Once you're seated, sit naturally without slouching in your chair or leaning on the desk. Throughout the interview, remember to smile frequently, maintain eye contact and not fidget.

Be clear: Answer all questions clearly and concisely, evidencing your most relevant skills, experiences and achievements. It's OK to pause before answering a difficult question to give yourself time to think, or to seek clarification if you don't understand what the question means. When answering, take your time and don't speak too quickly.

Show enthusiasm: Allow your personality to shine throughout the interview. Be curious and ask questions at appropriate moments. This will demonstrate that you're genuinely interested in the role and the interviewer.

Be memorable: Can you submit a document at the end of the interview? Maybe a three-month plan outlining what you'd like to achieve in the role? This would really show your enthusiasm and passion for the role, and would leave a positive lasting impression.

How to manage your nerves

It's completely natural to have some nerves before an interview, and nerves can be a positive thing – they can keep you focused and engaged. But what you don't want to do is allow your nerves to get the better of you and ruin your chances of securing your graduate job.

Here are some tips for keeping your nerves in check.

- Practise your responses to typical interview questions – get your family or friends to help you if you can.

- Remember that it's just a chat – an interview isn't an interrogation; it's a conversation.

- Remember that the interviewer wants you to succeed – they want to find the right person for the position.

- Don't forget to breathe – when you breathe deeply, your body relaxes and you're more in control of your thoughts and feelings.

- Don't worry about forgetting things – it's not a memory test; it's OK to take some prepared notes in with you (just don't read directly from a script).

I also recommend telling unique stories that convey your attributes. I can't tell you how many times I've heard students talk about their dissertation when I ask for an example of working under pressure. Most students will be able to give this example, so it doesn't stand out. Think about what you can talk about that will be more memorable.

As mentioned, it's OK to ask for a moment to think about the question if you're stuck. Think of it not as an interview but as a conversation about you – a topic you know all about. If you're feeling particularly nervous, remind yourself that the worst thing that could happen is you simply won't get the job. It's not the end of the world!

What to wear

Most assessment centres and job interviews are considered formal, so I recommend wearing a suit unless directed otherwise. You want to stand out for the right reasons, not your fashion sense. Keep your outfit simple and conservative – stick with grey, navy or black suits, and avoid bright, garish colours. When it comes to bags, shoes, ties, scarves and tights, it's best to play it safe. Keep these things muted and make sure they coordinate with your suit.

Tips for women:

- Don't overdo the jewellery
- Keep heels to an appropriate height (no more than 3 inches)
- Make sure you aren't showing too much cleavage
- Wear tights, even if it's summer
- If you wear a dress, make sure it's smart and mostly one solid colour

- Keep make-up and nail varnish subtle and understated

Tips for men:

- Ties should be low-key (avoid comedic or character prints)

- Choose a plain shirt – white, pale blue or light grey are the most appropriate – and make sure it's ironed

- Fasten the top button of your shirt and keep your tie knot tight to your neck

- Wear black shoes and coordinate with a matching belt (these will go well with any traditional suit colour)

- Ensure your suit fits you well – there's nothing worse than wearing a suit that's two times too big and looks like your older brother's hand-me-down

(Ignore the above advice if you're applying for a job in a creative industry such as fashion or design. In this case, you'll be expected to stand out for your fashion and be on trend, so grab your Vivienne Westwood or Alexander McQueen.)

Yes, I know the more formal approach sounds a little boring and conventional, but it's your personality that needs to shine through at the interview, not your clothing. Whatever the industry, always check with the employer if you're unsure. It's far better to ask and be prepared than to feel totally uncomfortable and out of place. This will put you off your game and make you stand out for all the wrong reasons.

Ghosting

You may be familiar with the term 'ghosting' in relation to dating, but the term is now used within recruitment too. It refers to that frustrating wall of silence you might hit at any stage of the recruitment process. This silence can be particularly frustrating if you've invested a lot of time with one employer and have made it through their entire process to the point where you're just waiting to hear if you actually have the job. There could be a number of reasons why you haven't heard back – for graduate roles, there are usually a number of assessment centres, and the employer can't make an offer until the last one has finished. Earlier on in the process, they might have a huge backlog of applications to get through. And from time to time, business priorities change at short notice – hiring plans might get frozen for the sake of cost-cutting.

The best thing you can do is to be patient. If it really has been a long time since you heard from the employer, and especially if they said you would hear back from them by a certain time, send a short and polite email to ask when you're likely to hear from them, reiterating that you're keen to secure the role but also stating that you're managing other applications.

What if you didn't get a job offer?

It can be hugely disappointing not to receive a job offer, especially if you have your heart set on working for one particular employer and/or you made it to the end of the recruitment process and were feeling confident. Sometimes it's just a matter of luck, and in a year where they had more vacancies, you would have been one of the lucky ones.

Even though your ego might be bruised and your confidence might have taken a knock, the best thing you can do is request feedback. If you make it to the last stage of the process, most employers will provide you with feedback on request. (Earlier in the process, they might not provide feedback or they might offer something generic.) Feedback will help you work out where you can develop and what you can improve.

Here are two distinct examples of reactions to being unsuccessful.

Paul was unsuccessful at the assessment-centre stage. His final score was about average, if I was comparing him to the other candidates, and our business only offered to the top 10% for this particular scheme, as we had limited places. Instead of politely asking me for feedback, which I would have gladly given him, he decided to complain to the MD of the whole company. Not only did this annoy me, but what did he expect the MD to do? The MD's secretary sent me the email to respond to, and although I gave him feedback, the outcome didn't change. Interestingly, I mentioned this incident to some other retail employers, and two of them had come across Paul and had had similar experiences with him. I spotted Paul at a national careers fair the following year, so he was still trying to secure a job.

Lizzie took a different approach. She was unsuccessful at the online test stage and got in contact with me. She'd connected with me on LinkedIn after meeting me at a careers fair. She explained how disappointed she was to be rejected at such an early stage and asked if she could meet with me to get some feedback and advice on how to improve her application for next time. We met for a coffee at my hotel when I was running an assessment centre in Manchester a few weeks later. I gave her the feedback, which was limited, as she had failed at such an early stage.

Lizzie came across as genuine and wanted to reapply the following year with my advice. Due to her positive approach and a little bit of serendipity, I ended up inviting her to an assessment centre for a placement programme I was trialling. I didn't tell any of the assessors her backstory, so she was treated like every other candidate. My hunch that she was worth a punt paid off, as she was the highest-scoring candidate by a mile. I offered her a placement position which converted to a graduate role and I'm pleased to report that Lizzie is still with the business today as a senior manager – a great result all round.

It's time to consider your options. Are there still schemes and jobs which you can apply for? If yes, and they're of interest, get back into the application process, armed with your feedback. You might decide to take a break, get a casual job or go travelling – and what you do during this time could provide some excellent experience to share the next time you apply for a graduate job or scheme. You can reapply to most graduate schemes the following year. I've met candidates who were unsuccessful but came back the following year and were offered a position. Resilience is a key skill that employers look for, and reapplying gives you an opportunity to highlight how you bounced back after a disappointment.

EXPERT INSIGHT

'The most important advice is to stick with it: job hunting requires persistence. It might help if you can make the process less isolating – find friends who are in the same boat and have regular "job search" catch-ups to share experiences, practise your interview techniques and provide encouragement. Visit your careers service – perhaps another pair of eyes will spot something about your CV or the examples you use in interviews that's holding you back. At the end of the day, a job search is a bit of a numbers game: there will be plenty of applicants for each vacancy, so how do you make sure yours stands out from the crowd? Building up experience that makes you distinctive, learning to tell your story in an engaging manner, and doing your research to make sure your application is tailored to a specific vacancy will eventually help you take the first step on the path to the career you want.' (Gary)

Part Two Summary

To secure a job offer, you need a lot of time, energy, patience and, most importantly, preparation. Find the time to use the resources available to you – especially practice tests and feedback and guidance from experts. At all stages of recruitment, you need to showcase yourself and your understanding of the organisation.

The STARR technique is widely used precisely because it's the best way to convey your key achievements. Aim to show how your achievements or skills are relevant, of value to the employer and, wherever possible, original. You should also go one step further by using the vocabulary or referencing values that are important to your employer.

And as cliched as it sounds, be yourself. It's your unique personality and strengths that will be of most interest to employers. Does your CV reflect you as a person or is it just full of technical skills, generic examples and stock phrases? How can you show your personal brand through your online presence?

Finally, I want to reiterate the importance of resilience. If you aren't successful in an exercise, or in the whole process, learn from the experience and move on. Employers are increasingly looking and testing for this strength. Be resilient, be prepared, be you and secure a fantastic graduate job.

PART THREE
IMPRESSING IN YOUR

'The results you achieve will be in direct proportion
to the effort you apply.'
— Denis Waitley

Ten
Managing Offers

Finally, you get the news you've been waiting for. All your hard work has paid off. You have an offer or, if you're really lucky, several offers on the table. Nothing can quite prepare you for the words 'we'd like to offer you the job'. But before you jump in and sign on the dotted line, it's important to take some time to consider the offer and respond appropriately.

EXPERT INSIGHT

'Doing a disappearing act, ie not responding to calls, messages and emails and then dropping out the week before is unimpressive. We don't mind people dropping out – we know it happens, but it's important to do it professionally and in good time so organisations can plan around this.' (David)

How to respond professionally to an offer

You need to consider several factors before jumping straight into accepting your offer, particularly if you have a few applications pending. Maybe this offer isn't the one you really want, and your top offer is yet to be confirmed.

The important thing is to take your time. Your head is likely to be buzzing with excitement at the thought of your new role (and potentially your new life), but you need to stop and take a breath and give yourself some time to process the information before confirming your decision.

When replying, ensure you express your enthusiasm for the offer and show interest. Here's an appropriate response:

> 'Thank you very much for the offer. I want to stress how excited I am about the role and your organisation; however, I'm still waiting for the outcomes following my other interviews. Would it be possible to have some time, so I can fully consider this offer?'

Most graduate employers will understand your desire to take time to consider the offer. Just make sure you reply within a suitable time frame. For example, if the employer gives you two weeks to think about it, contact them within that time, otherwise they may retract the offer.

Accepting an offer

Usually a verbal offer over the telephone will be followed up by a formal offer letter. This letter will include things such as:

- Job title
- Department
- Salary and benefits
- Start date
- Other terms and conditions

If you're happy with the terms and conditions, you can accept the offer by email or telephone or in writing.

It's important to withdraw from any other application processes you're still involved in at this point, as a courtesy to other employers and candidates.

Juggling multiple offers

If you're lucky enough to find yourself in a position where you have to decide which offer to choose, consider these questions:

- What makes each job/organisation different?
- What's your order of preference?
- What are the offers and how do they compare?

Consider what feels right about each organisation. Do you prefer its values and culture? Perhaps the location is good? Maybe it has better development opportunities? As mentioned, it's OK to ask employers for some time, so you can decide which offer is best for you. Just don't take too long, because unless you have already made the employer aware of a specific timeline, you might find the opportunity has been given to someone else. And don't play organisations off against each other. This isn't professional and will damage your credibility and reputation.

TASK: Decision matrix analysis

In a decision matrix analysis, you list your options as rows on a table and the factors you need to consider as columns. You then score each option-factor combination, weight this score by the relative importance of the factor and add these scores up to create an overall score for each option.

While this sounds complex, this technique is quite easy to use. Simply work through these steps and see the example decision matrix analysis below.

Step 1

List all your options as the row labels on the table and list the factors that you need to consider as the column headings. For example, factors to consider might be salary, cost of living at the job location, development opportunities offered by the company, benefits (eg gym membership, holiday allowance, company reputation) and anything else that matters to you.

Step 2

Work your way down the columns, scoring each factor from 0 (poor) to 4 (very good). You don't have to have a different score for each option – all options could score 0 if none of them are good.

Step 3

Work out the relative importance of the factors in your decision. Show these as numbers from 0 to 4, where 0 means that the factor is absolutely unimportant in the final decision and 4 means that it's very important. (Again, it's perfectly acceptable to have factors with the same importance.)

Step 4

Multiply each of your scores from step 2 by the value of the factor's relative importance that you calculated in step 3. This will give you weighted scores for each option-factor combination.

Step 5

Add up these weighted scores for each of your options. The option that scores the highest wins. If your intuition tells you that the top-scoring option isn't the best one, then reflect on the scores and weightings. This may be a sign that certain factors are more important to you than you initially thought.

Example of a decision matrix analysis

Factors in your decision		Salary	Cost of living	Development opportunities	Benefits	Total
Score 0 (poor) to 4 (very good)	Job offer A	2	2	4	2	10
	Job offer B	4	3	4	1	12
	Job offer C	1	2	3	3	9
Relative importance of each factor Score 0 (poor) to 4 (very good)		3	2	4	1	
Weighted score Multiply factors to consider by relative importance	Job offer A	6	4	16	2	28
	Job offer B	12	6	16	1	35
	Job offer C	3	4	12	3	22

STUDENT CASE STUDY: SHERIF, UNIVERSITY OF NOTTINGHAM

'I was offered three jobs in the spring of my final year. I felt so lucky! I decided to ask each employer if I could meet with them to ask a few questions, and all accepted my suggestion. I met with each employer at their head office and brought a list of questions with me. I immediately got a better feel for each organisation just by spending time in their office and observing their employees. Asking the questions helped to clarify my understanding of each graduate scheme, and it became easier to make my decision.'

Declining an offer

EXPERT INSIGHT

Matt had a situation where a candidate to whom they had offered a full-time grad role returned his signed offer letter. 'The issue was that it was his signed offer letter for one of our competitors – a novel way of letting us know he was declining us.' (Matt)

If you decide to decline an offer, contact the organisation as soon as possible, so they can make alternative arrangements to fill the position. There may be an opportunity to work for them in the future, so ensure that you leave them with a positive impression. Always be polite and professional and thank them for the opportunity. It's a small world – you never know if your paths will cross again.

How to successfully negotiate your pay and benefits

As if getting through the interview process wasn't terrifying enough – now you may have to think about negotiating your pay and benefits. Clearly defined starting salaries and benefits will likely be set out at the beginning of the application process, but if you find yourself in a place where you can negotiate (perhaps with an SME), here are a few things to consider:

- Know the market – look at other graduate roles in the field and see how the salary compares
- Be realistic and manage your own expectations
- Think beyond salary and consider the benefits package you're being offered. Some benefits that may be included are:
  - Annual leave
  - Bonus schemes
  - Relocation costs
  - Flexible working
  - Travel schemes
  - Healthcare
  - Pension
  - Gym membership
  - Subsidised meals

Your employer is likely to have a figure in mind for your salary, but don't simply accept or reject the first offer.

- Ask if there's any flexibility in the offer, as well as how regularly salary reviews will take place –

taking a lower salary will be more acceptable if there will be regular salary reviews.

- If the salary is lower than your minimum expectation, explain that the offer is below what you were expecting, backing this up with why.

- If the package is around your expected salary, you should still attempt negotiation – explain how your experience, knowledge and qualifications position you in the market.

- If you're offered your dream salary, discuss room for future growth in earnings and career development; remember, although this is your dream salary, as you progress, your expectations are likely to increase.

What to do between receiving your offer and starting the job

You may be so excited to get an offer that you immediately want to accept. The role may mean working for your ideal business in an exciting role, but you must nevertheless take time to reflect on the details of the offer.

Checklist for accepting an offer

In your offer letter and during your negotiations, make sure that the following questions are addressed.

If they aren't, contact the employer to find out the answers.

- What job role am I being offered?
- What salary is being offered?
- Where will I be working from?
- If the role requires relocation, what costs will be involved in this?
- When will I start?
- What are my working hours?
- What annual-leave entitlement is offered?
- What pension contribution does the employer make?
- What probation or notice periods are there?
- How and when is performance reviewed?
- What additional benefits are there?

Once you've accepted the job, keep in touch with your new employer. They may have additional paperwork for you to complete, or they may want you to meet with your manager and/or team before you start.

Do your research

You may think the days of studying and researching are over, but now it's important to prepare yourself for your new role and the organisation. Talk to your employer to find out if there's anything you can do in advance.

- Is there any reading to do regarding the position, industry or organisation?

- Who are the competitors to research?

- What industry publications might be worth reading?

- Does the induction require you to complete anything in your own time, such as mandatory training?

Get organised

Consider using the time before you start to get organised, using the pointers below.

- Think about the things you might need when you start work, such as stationery or other equipment.

- Know the dress code and make sure you have the right clothing.

- Organise travel arrangements and plan your route.

- Know which documents you need to take with you on your first day.

- Think about what you're going to do for lunch – will you take something with you or buy it there?

Most importantly, make the most of your time off before you start. Plan a short break away or enjoy time with friends and family. This time is precious, so make the most of it.

STUDENT CASE STUDY: ANNIKA, LEEDS BECKETT UNIVERSITY

'I had about four months off between finishing uni and starting my graduate job. I used some of this time to go travelling, which was an amazing experience. I also attended a couple of events run by my new employer when I was back in the UK. In my free time, I kept up to date with the news as there was lots going on with the economy which was relevant to my new employer and I wanted to be clued-up ahead of starting. I bought some new work outfits the week before I started and did a couple of trials on different transport routes, so I was organised for day one. Being prepared gave me confidence for my first day.'

EXPERT INSIGHT

'Being proactive between accepting the offer and starting the job stands out. Don't wait for the organisation to do all the work – within the retail space we often saw successful applicants wanting to pick up part-time roles in stores so that they really felt connected to and had an awareness of the heart of the organisation before joining.' (Helen)

Eleven
The Transition Into The World Of Work

It can be challenging to transition from university into the world of work. Moving from studying and exam revision to a full-time job is a big change, and for graduates who haven't been employed before, this can be a big culture shock!

Making a great first impression

It's important to start as you mean to go on in your new job. There are a few things you can do on your first day and beyond to impress your new employers.

Arrive on time

It's always better to be early than it is to be late. Leave yourself plenty of time and consider your travel arrangements and how long it will take you to get to work in rush hour. There's nothing worse than using the 'the bus was late' excuse in your first week!

Dress appropriately

Never underestimate the importance of dressing appropriately. The way that you dress can impact your first impression greatly. Most organisations adhere to one of these three dress codes (do your research to find out which one your organisation follows):

- **Business professional** (banking and financial services): A business suit, shirt or blouse, tie, formal shoes

- **Business casual or smart casual** (marketing and engineering): Smart chinos or trousers with a shirt and shoes

- **Comfy casual** (creative industries): Jeans, T-shirt and trainers

Be positive

Nothing says 'I'm pleased to be joining' more than having a positive and can-do attitude. Show enthusiasm for being part of the team and meet new people. Leave any personal problems to one side and channel your passion into this new opportunity.

Ask questions or for help if you need it

No one expects you to know everything on your first day, and you may find that it takes weeks or even months until you feel comfortable with everything. Enjoy the first few weeks of being new and ask lots of questions – this shows your interest and that you care about doing things right. And it's far better to ask for help than plough on with a task and make mistakes that you could have avoided.

Make notes and stay organised

You'll likely attend an induction programme – make lots of notes. Listen to what's said about the culture and any processes or rules that they may have. Keep a diary or make a to-do list to help you stay organised. You'll be surprised by how much information you receive in your first few weeks, so help your brain out and make some notes to refer to later, should you need reminding of something.

EXPERT INSIGHT
'Immerse yourself in the organisation – get involved with as much as possible. An early careers role is the ideal opportunity to act like a sponge and develop a

huge amount. Those who grasp responsibility, grasp the opportunity etc tend to progress quicker, in my experience.' (David)

How to behave in the workplace

Different organisations will have different cultures and expectations. Often, there are unwritten rules about how to behave in a particular workplace, so it's important to observe your colleagues and the organisation to see what's acceptable and what isn't.

When it comes to trying to understand workplace culture, the best things you can do are:

- Read the company handbook, policies, procedures and rules

- Observe interactions and relationships between colleagues, managers and leaders

Ask questions and be curious. I've outlined some key things to think about:

Observe workplace etiquette

It's important to remember your manners, and I'm not just talking about your 'pleases' and 'thank yous'. If you can use a mobile phone at work, make sure it doesn't distract you or your colleagues. If you have an office phone, don't receive or make personal calls on it – use it only for business calls.

This also goes for your work email. Keep it professional and use your personal email only during break times or in your own time.

Admit your mistakes

It's human nature to make mistakes, and at some point in your career, you'll make one. And it might be a whopper! Just remember that mistakes happen to the best of us. Often, how you handle the mistake is far more important than the mistake itself, so always admit when you've made a mistake and don't ignore it or try to blame someone else. Take full responsibility and look for ways to fix the mistake. And if in doubt, always ask for help.

Respect your colleagues

Respect in the workplace is extremely important. Colleagues who respect each other tend to get along well – and no boss wants their employees arguing and fighting. Always be polite and professional and avoid unnecessary conflict or drama. Do the things you've agreed to do, share the workload and never take credit for someone else's work.

Represent your employer well

Whether you're attending a meeting, a conference, an event or a work lunch or night out, remember that you're representing your employer. Dress appropriately and manage your intake of alcohol (and if you can't – don't drink!). Always remain professional. And should other colleagues be unable to attend the events, be willing to share information and what you learned on your return.

Avoid office politics and gossip

The workplace can be full of rumours and gossip, and it can be difficult not to get involved. Try to keep your distance from the office gossips! Every workplace has one. Remain neutral on work-related topics during your first few weeks. It's OK to have an opinion, but make sure it's well thought through and adds value!

EXPERT INSIGHTS

'Be proactive! Make a contribution, make an effort to get to know people and ask to get involved in projects, discussions and meetings early on rather than waiting to be told.' (Helen)

'Great candidates connected with all their management team on LinkedIn, for example. A candidate even got their academic professor to meet with the management team.' (Ashley)

Understand how your performance will be measured

The world of work brings new challenges, one of which is understanding what's expected of you. You'll need to understand how your performance will be measured. Unlike university, workplace performance isn't always black and white (ie pass or fail).

Know what's expected of you

You will hopefully have gained insight into the role while applying for your graduate job, but it's important to be clear on what your employer expects from you now. Expectations will encompass behaviour, quality of work, results, skills and competence and are usually set out in a performance management or appraisal process.

Build a relationship with your line manager

Agree with your line manager on how often you'll meet. This is your opportunity to discuss performance and will help keep your boss informed on how you're getting on. Together, you can work through any challenges you might be facing. Agree to specific dates and times and send a calendar invite. Your line manager will likely suggest this approach, but it doesn't hurt to be one step ahead of the game.

Set goals

Once you have a solid understanding of what's expected of you, you can set yourself goals and think about how you're going to work towards meeting the expectations of your line manager and the organisation.

Ask yourself these questions:

Identify

- What's important to me?

- What do I need to achieve?

- What are my strengths?

- What are my development areas?

Plan

- What resources are available to help me?

- When do I need to achieve these goals?

- Who will support me?

Take action and record

- What methods of learning are available?

- How will I achieve my goals?

- Who could coach or mentor me?

Review and reflect

- What have I learned?

- What could I do differently?

- What's next?

You can record your goals, objectives and areas for development using a personal development plan. This is an action plan to help you get from where you are to where you want to be.

You'll find a link to download a personal development plan at www.sophiemilliken.co.uk/from-learner-to-earner-resources.

Reflect on outcomes and evaluate achievements and progress. Review and re-establish future plans/goals

Self-assess skills and identify strengths and weaknesses

Develop your skills eg workshops, online course, seminars, self-study, conferences, mentoring, practice and more

Prioritise development needs in consultation with supervisor(s) and develop a plan of action

Longer-term career planning

Although you've probably been focused on getting your first graduate job, you've likely given some thought to what you want from your career long-term. There are good habits you can get into that will help you develop your career at pace and will help you succeed throughout your working life.

Record your accomplishments

When you start your graduate job, you'll likely be working on many different projects for many different teams. Fast forward to eight months in, you probably won't remember all your successes and achievements. If you start recording your successes now, they'll be easier to recall when you get to your performance review.

To download my 'Record your accomplishments' worksheet to help you record all your successes, visit www.sophiemilliken.co.uk/from-learner-to-earner-resources.

Get a mentor

Many CEOs have said to me that having a mentor had a significant impact on their careers. While you might not be aiming for the role of CEO initially, a mentor or buddy can be a sounding board who offers impartial and confidential guidance throughout the first months of your career. Based on insights from their own experiences, a mentor or buddy can help you:

- Prepare for cultural challenges in the workplace
- Deal with the learning curve
- Make the transition from school into the workplace
- Plan your career and set goals
- Identify opportunities to progress and develop your career
- Raise your profile within the organisation

It's important to find someone who:

- **Challenges you and your thinking:** A good mentor or buddy will always push you to be your best and not to shy away from opportunities to develop yourself.

- **Is experienced and credible:** Your mentor or buddy should have advice they can share with you that's based on real-life experiences.

- **Is where you want to be:** Choose a mentor or buddy who has the same vision of success as you.

- **Supports you:** A good mentor or buddy will offer guidance and pick you up if you fall.

- **Is good at listening:** A good mentor or buddy will listen and help you make your own decisions rather than just giving you their own opinion.

- **Is available:** A good mentor or buddy will make time to be available for you.

- **Respects you:** A good mentor or buddy will never look down on you or judge you.

- **Provides honest and constructive feedback:** Your mentor or buddy will celebrate your success but also offer honest feedback to help you.

- **Guides you towards the answer:** Your mentor or buddy should never just give you the answer but allow you the space to explore and figure it out for yourself.

- **Is invested in your success:** Your mentor or buddy will be happy to see you succeed and grow within your career.

Helpful tools to develop your career

SMARTER objectives

SMARTER is a well-established tool to help guide your goal setting. The acronym allows you to ensure that your goals are specific, measurable, achievable, realistic, timely, exciting and reviewable.

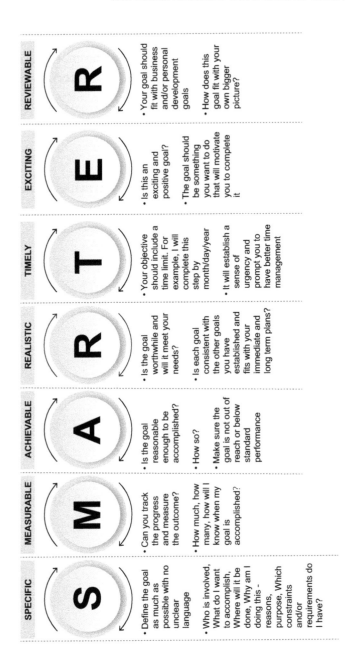

SPECIFIC — S
- Define the goal as much as possible with no unclear language
- Who is involved, What do I want to accomplish, Where will it be done, Why am I doing this – reasons, purpose, Which constraints and/or requirements do I have?

MEASURABLE — M
- Can you track the progress and measure the outcome?
- How much, how many, how will I know when my goal is accomplished?

ACHIEVABLE — A
- Is the goal reasonable enough to be accomplished?
- How so?
- Make sure the goal is not out of reach or below standard performance

REALISTIC — R
- Is the goal worthwhile and will it meet your needs?
- Is each goal consistent with the other goals you have established and fits with your immediate and long term plans?

TIMELY — T
- Your objective should include a time limit. For example, I will complete this step by month/day/year
- It will establish a sense of urgency and prompt you to have better time management

EXCITING — E
- Is this an exciting and positive goal?
- The goal should be something you want to do that will motivate you to complete it

REVIEWABLE — R
- Your goal should fit with business and/or personal development goals
- How does this goal fit with your own bigger picture?

197

When you use this tool, you create clear, attainable and worthwhile goals and you have the motivation and support to achieve them. For more information on this, please refer to Chapter Two.

Career development plan

A career development plan will help you achieve your career goals, and a clear direction within your career will also help you grow and develop personally.

A career development plan helps you break down long-term goals into manageable steps. This way, it's easier to stay on track and keep focused.

Five reasons to have a career development plan

A career development plan can help you:

1. Take ownership of your career path

2. Define your purpose and passions

3. Identify your strengths and where best to apply these

4. Not to get stuck in a rut

5. Be in control of your destiny

To download a career development plan to help you plan your short- and long-term career goals, visit www.sophiemilliken.co.uk/from-learner-to-earner-resources.

MY TOP TIP

Don't forget to remain active on LinkedIn even when you aren't actively looking for a new job. It's a good habit to update your profile at least monthly to keep track of new achievements and ensure your details are current. Many people use LinkedIn daily as a networking tool and to keep their industry knowledge fresh. And your being active on LinkedIn will come in handy when you do consider a new job.

Part Three Summary

Whether you're declining an offer or starting a new job, the golden rule applies: treat others as you want to be treated. Aim to be professional, positive and, most importantly, open and honest. By talking to your employer about what you enjoy and what you're struggling with, you'll help them to provide the best experience and get the best from you.

Give yourself time. Take time to ensure that you're making the right decision – consider what kind of impact the job will have on your life. Spend time getting to know the employer, both before and after you join the organisation. Ultimately, this will help you start a new chapter feeling positive and confident. And give yourself time to adjust to what's an enormous change and reflect upon what you're learning.

And even if you've just started your graduate job, prepare for the future by logging your achievements and creating a personal development plan. These things can provide structure and meaning when you may be feeling lost or outside your comfort zone.

There will likely be a lot to learn and do, but enjoy yourself and remember that the expert in anything was once a beginner.

Final Thoughts

It's now time to put your learning into practice. By reading this book, you've already developed your knowledge of the graduate labour market far beyond the understanding of most students. This knowledge will guide you to apply for jobs at the best time to maximise your chances of success as well as identify employers you might not have previously considered (such as an SME, for example). You know all the right ways to contact employers as part of your job research and are aware of the value that one strong encounter can bring.

Having clarified what you value and given some thought to what the employer can offer you, you now have a better understanding of which jobs you're most likely to enjoy and can narrow your search so that you submit only high-quality applications.

Identifying what you actually want to do and which jobs to apply for can be a huge task, but the main hurdle is successfully navigating the application process and earning a job offer or two. By implementing the advice in Part Two and completing the tasks, you'll have a strong CV, cover letter and LinkedIn profile ready to impress employers. You'll be prepared for the various tests you might encounter and know where to go to practise these. The STARR model can help you put together a strong application form that will get you through to the next round.

At telephone or video interview stage, you'll know what not to do and how to impress to secure an invite to the assessment centre. Assessment centres can be daunting but knowing what to expect from them can alleviate nerves. You know the types of exercises you'll likely need to complete and have an idea of what will score well. The STARR model comes back into play during final interviews – it will help you construct strong and interesting responses to any questions.

Getting a job offer is the end game, but Part Three has given you the knowledge to develop lifelong career-development skills that will enable you to progress in your career at a faster pace than your peers. Don't underestimate the power of a strong and current LinkedIn profile. Make use of the tools in this final section – record your progress and highlight your success.

I wish you so much luck in your job search and would love to hear about your success.

Resources

You can download all of the resources referred to in this book from www.sophiemilliken.co.uk/from-learner-to-earner-resources.

For a reminder of what is available, the resources are listed below in the order that they appear in the book.

Part One

Early career plan

Goal-setting worksheet

Job-search planner

Part Two

Step-by-step guide to setting up your LinkedIn profile

Action words to help write your profile

Skills worksheet

CV templates

Cover letter templates

Question preparation using STARR worksheet

Competency-based example questions

Strengths-based example questions

Part Three

Personal development plan

Record your accomplishments worksheet

Career development plan

Acknowledgements

I would like to thank everyone who has helped me with this book. At Rethink Press, Lucy McCarraher helped me to develop my initial idea and, along with Kathy Steeden, worked with me at pace, offering lots of advice and encouragement to keep me on track.

I am grateful to the many graduate recruiters who have contributed with examples and stories from their own experiences with students. Particular thanks must go to Helen Alkin, Ashley Hever, Tonia Galati, Gary Argent, Paul Roberts, Phillipa Chakhtoura, Matthew Parker and David Gawthorpe.

I want to thank my team at Smart Resourcing Solutions, who deliver outstanding service to our clients every day and have also provided exceptional support and patience during the writing of this book. Special thanks go to Rachael Cook for her brilliant graphic skills in the presentation of data within the book and Helen Liddle for carrying out my numerous research requests and providing valuable feedback at each stage.

For the use of survey data, I would like to thank the ISE, HECSU, Charlie Ball, Prospects Luminate and High Fliers Research.

And finally, thanks to the thousands of students I have met over the years at our university events. Seeing students develop their confidence and skills never gets boring and remains a constant source of energy.

The Author

As a former graduate recruiter at John Lewis and now working with a variety of employers and universities as managing director at graduate recruitment and employability consultancy Smart Resourcing Solutions, Sophie Milliken is a recruitment and employability expert.

She introduced a number of new graduate and placement schemes at John Lewis, steering the retailer to multi-award-winning success and to achieve a number-nine position in *The Times Top 100 Graduate Employers* list.

She has worked with employers such as M&S, JP Morgan, Expedia and AXA to design and deliver their graduate recruitment campaigns. Her company is also the leading provider of assessment-centre simulations for universities and has trained over 20,000 students at these events.

Sophie has been a Fellow of the Chartered Institute of Personnel and Development since 2013 and was awarded a Fellowship of the Royal Society of Arts in 2019. Her MSc in HR Management and Level 7 Certificate in Leadership Coaching and Mentoring lend further credibility to her expertise.

It's Sophie's passion to see every student and graduate being given the skills and knowledge they need to secure a fantastic job after university that drives much of the work she does and has led to writing this book.

You can contact her through her website or via social media at:

🐦 @SRS_Sophie

in www.linkedin.com/in/sophie-milliken

⊕ www.sophiemilliken.co.uk

f www.facebook.com/SRSSophie

⊙ srs_sophie